Acting in the Million Dollar Minute

The Art and Business of Performing in TV Commercials

Tom Logan

Communications Press
Washington, D.C.

Grateful acknowledgment is made to the American Federation of Television and Radio Artists (AFTRA) for permission to reprint the lists of its locals and chapters; to the Screen Actors Guild (SAG) for permission to reprint the list of its offices; to the following actors for permission to reprint their photographs: Lillian Adams, Teresa Brown, Blake Higgins, Phil Mann, and Morgan Webb; to the photographers: Olivier de Courson, Buddy Rosenberg, Tama Rothschild, and Kirby Sires; and to Anderson Graphics for its design and graphics presentation of the composite. Grateful acknowledgement also is made to Leo Burnett Company, Inc., Kellogg Company, and Procter & Gamble Productions, Inc., for permission to reprint their commercial scripts, and to the Lever Brothers Company for permission to reprint their Promise® commercial storyboard.

ISBN 0-89461-041-4

Cover design by Linda McKnight

Printed in the United States of America

Communications Press
  a division of
Broadcasting Publications Inc.
1705 DeSales Street, N.W.
Washington, D.C. 20036

First Printing June 1984
Second Printing September 1985
Third Printing April 1987
Fourth Printing May 1988

Library of Congress Cataloging in Publication Data

Logan, Tom.
  Acting in the million dollar minute.

  1. Acting for television—Vocational guidance. 2. Television advertising—Vocational guidance. I. Title.
PN1992.8.A3L6 1984   791.43'028'02373   84-12048   ISBN 0-89461-041-4

This book is dedicated to my nieces and nephews, Shelly & Todd Abbiatti, and Lisa & Paul Logan, for the sunshine they have brought into my life.

Contents

Acknowledgments . . . . *vii*

Introduction 1

Part One   **The *Art* of Acting in Commercials** 5

Chapter 1   **Basic Principles** 7
*Frame of Reference, Observation, Memory
Substitution*

Chapter 2   **Terminology and Procedure** 17
*Script Terms—Types of Shots, Other Script
Terms; The Storyboard; How a Commercial Is Shot*

Chapter 3   **Commercial Dialogue** 28
*Reading, Analyzing the Script, Coloring Words,
Transitions, Pacing the Copy, Speaking from
the Script or Q-Cards, Projection, Relating to
Your Partner*

Chapter 4   **Basic Camera Staging** 41
*Standing, Sitting, Kneeling, Walking, Hitting
Marks, Crossing in Front of Someone, Head
Movement, Eyes, Smiling, Gesturing, Working
with the Set*

Chapter 5   **The Hero** 58
*Using Substitution, Mentioning the Product
Name, Putting the Product in Its Best Light,
Handling the Product*

Part Two   The *Business* of Acting in Commercials 63

Chapter 6   **Getting Started** 65
Training, Photos, The Resume

Chapter 7   **Obtaining an Agent** 85
The Big Search, The Agent Interview

Chapter 8   **Unions and Agency Contracts** 94
*Unions, Actor-Agency Contracts, Escape
Clauses, Changing Agents*

Chapter 9   **The Commercial Interview** 103
*Where Agents Don't Exist, Preparing for the
Interview, Beginning of the Interview, Before
the Screen Test, The Screen Test, After the Screen
Test, Call Backs, After the Interview*

Chapter 10   **Pay and Working Conditions** 117
*Union Commercials—Basic Pay, Interviews,
Commercials, Product Conflict, Wardrobe, Meals,
Location Shooting, Rest Periods Between Days,
Overtime; Nonunion Commercials*

Finale 127

    Appendices
A. Commercial Scripts for Practice 133
B. Offices of SAG and AFTRA 165
C. Other Avenues for Making Money 171

About the Author 175

Acknowledgments

A great many people—too many to name here—have helped me develop my craft. For all their aid and encouragement, deep thanks are due. And specific credits are due to individuals and organizations that contributed to the production of this book as follows:

Grateful acknowledgement is made to the following actors for use of their photographs: Lillian Adams, Teresa Brown, Morgan Webb, Phil Mann, and Blake Higgins; to the photographers: Olivier de Courson, Buddy Rosenberg, Kirby Sires, and Tama Rothschild; and a special thanks to Anderson Graphics for its design and graphics presentation of the composite, and to Linda McKnight for her wonderful illustrations and cover design.

Also, acknowledgment is made to the Leo Burnett Company, Inc., and two of its clients, the Kellogg Company and Procter & Gamble Productions, Inc. for providing the commercial scripts used in the appendices, and to the Lever Brothers Company for the storyboard used herein.

A special thanks to Kat Krone and John Kunsak of the Screen Actors Guild contracts department for their hours of explanations of guild contracts, and a very, very special thanks to Mark Locher, assistant information director of the Screen Actors Guild, for his continued help, energy, encouragement, and friendship.

This book also benefited from the considerable production skills contributed by Charlie Todd of C.W. Type and Judy Smith of Soleil Associates. And last, but certainly not least, the driving force behind my book—Communications Press. Thanks to David Dietz for his editorial assistance. And especially to Executive Editor and Publisher of Communications Press, Mary Louise Hollowell, for her incredible editorial guidance and relentless drive for accuracy, and for being a downright all-around nice lady!

Introduction

Perhaps TV commercials have given you a little more information than you care to know about the digestive tract, designer jeans, dirty collars, youthful skin, light beer, and lost traveler's checks. I'm with you. After watching a series of TV commercials, I sometimes suffer headache, nausea, and skin rashes from the overdose. But, were it not for Avon calling and Revlon answering, our free TV and radio media could not exist.

And, frankly, no matter how much we may complain about TV commercials, plenty of us *do* respond to them. Why else would a company pay $150,000 to $800,000 for one minute of network air time during a prime viewing period? With so much money spent for a *single airing* of a commercial which may run many times, you know the company is going to spend a lot of money on developing a commercial that *works* when it gets on the air.

A little background on how the commercial comes into being:

Suppose a particular national company invents a new product or service, or wishes to improve sales of one of its products already on the market. The company hires an advertising agency to create a TV campaign that will be successful, the company hopes, in getting this product out to the American public if it's a new product, or bolstering its sales if it's an old one.

The client (company hiring the ad agency) will then meet with the ad agency to discuss the campaign (i.e., inform the agency about its ideas concerning the campaign). The ad agency works on the campaign based on that general meeting with the client.

When completed, the campaign plan is presented to the client. Usually, many more meetings take place between the client and the ad agency before the client is satisfied with the campaign and the actual shooting script.

When the campaign has been approved by the client, the ad agency hires a producer—a person in charge of the actual shooting—and a production house to shoot the commercial. It is at this point that casting occurs. A number of people—casting director, director, producer, ad agency representatives, and the client—may be responsible for the casting. After all considerations, it is the client who has the final say on which actor(s) will perform in the commercial. (Locally, commercials tend to work in the same basic way, though sometimes the merchant himself will perform many of the tasks described here.)

This thumbnail sketch of how a commercial production comes into being should demonstrate to you that a lot of careful thought and preparation has been put into a commercial script before an actor sees it. Much attention has been paid to every detail.

All this discussion of the importance, cost, and development of commercials brings us to you—THE COMMERCIAL ACTOR. *You* are the center of this important world of advertising. *You* will sell the product or service. Companies depend on *you* the actor to get their messages across to the public. *Your* credibility alone could determine the success or failure of the company sponsoring the commercial! The importance of *you* is the reason I have written this book.

The general public has the idea that actors in commercials aren't really acting. This couldn't be further from the truth. Commercial acting is one of the toughest acting jobs you might ever have. In a commercial you must take a few hours', days', or weeks' time and compress them into a believable sixty seconds or less. There is no time for character development. The dialogue won't be everyday real-life dialogue. You won't have the freedom to choose your rhythm, because the commercial will have to be delivered in a specific amount of time. And, you must create a likeable character with which the public can identify.

When you see a commercial on TV, you might think to yourself, "Well . . . . they just picked that person off the street. Anyone can do that." Or maybe you see another one, and think, "Hey, I can be that obnoxious (or earnest, thrilled, snobby, or whatever), too." But *can* you create that appropriate impression, without any artistic and technical training and preparation?

We the public may assume that the people in those consumer interview ads, for example, are just cornered by an interviewer at the local shopping mall, that their responses are off-the-cuff, and that they've never been on TV before. In actuality they may be experienced actors speaking from a prepared script. Rarely is a person simply picked off the street and put into a commercial. The actor playing the part is giving you that illusion. That's a credit to his performance. FOLKS, COMMERCIAL ACTING AIN'T EASY! But you can do it.

Since you are reading my book, I am going to assume that you are ready to stop just toying with the idea of being in a commercial yourself, and to get serious about it. But this book is only the beginning. You can't learn to act by reading, any more than you can learn to snow-ski by reading. You can get a good understanding of what the process is to act or ski by reading, but when you get in front of the camera or on the slopes, you'll find that it is different from what you originally thought.

WHAT THIS BOOK WILL GIVE YOU IS A BASIC UNDERSTANDING OF WHAT COMMERCIAL ACTING PRINCIPLES AND TECHNIQUES SELL AND HOW TO SELL THEM. It's important for you to know the basics. Then when you start auditioning (known in industry jargon as "interviewing") for commercial acting jobs, you'll know the principles set forth in this book and how to apply them. The *application* is the most important aspect of your reading **Acting in the Million Dollar Minute.**

This book is divided into two sections. Part One is on the ART of acting in commercials. After laying down some general acting principles, it defines the lingo and explains the techniques of shooting; outlines principles for dealing with dialogue; describes staging techniques—providing tips on how to use your body; and then concentrates on dialogue and staging with the *product specifically*. To help you practice what you learn in Part One, I've included as an appendix to this book several commercial scripts from actual ad campaigns, furnished by the Leo Burnett Company, Inc.

Part Two is on the BUSINESS. It gives practical instructions on getting started—training, photos, resume, finding an agent, and dealing with that agent; advises on business matters such as contracts, escape clauses, changing agents, and unions; and tells you how to handle the commercial interview from the sign-in when you enter to the thank-you notes you send after you leave.

Part One

The *Art* of Acting in Commercials

First of all, let's discuss what I believe to be the most important trait an actor needs to make it in the professional acting business—CONFIDENCE. I don't care how talented you are or aren't, you will go nowhere in this business if your "head isn't in the right place."

When you walk into a producer's, agent's, or casting director's office, he will immediately begin sizing you up. If you walk into that office with the attitude that you can't do the job, then he knows you can't do the job. After all, you know yourself better than he does, and he will sense the negative vibes you send out about your ability as an actor.

Let's put it this way: if you were about to get onto the freeway and you kept thinking to yourself, "I just know I'm going to have a wreck," you would actually enhance your chances of having an accident. The more you tell yourself something, the more it tends to become reality for you. Psychologists have found that if they tell a person he has a low IQ, that person will tend to perform less intelligently. This tendency is so strong that it's against school board rules in many states to reveal to students what their IQ scores are. When someone believes something wholeheartedly about himself, he will tend to act in ways to support that belief.

So, right from the start, make sure that your attitude is such that you know you will do well in the commercial acting profession. You're going to walk into the interviews with such confidence that commercial agents, casting directors, directors, and producers will believe in you and be happy to hire your services.

I have been acting in TV commercials for many years. The chapters which follow contain tips and techniques I have picked up from that experience. I would never have had the opportunity to learn what you are about to read if I had not believed in my ability to succeed. If you read Part One of this book carefully, you will have a definite advantage over the untutored novice. Keep that in mind—and believe in yourself!

Chapter One

Basic Principles

You walk into an acting class in smog-filled Los Angeles with high hopes of creating and developing your acting skills. You look around the room sizing up the other students. You wonder how much training they have had. Finally this twirpy little guy who looks like the type you'd see on the "Newlywed Game" walks into the class and introduces himself as your teacher.

He takes a pencil out of his pocket and tosses it on the floor in front of you and tells you to concentrate very hard on that pencil. He wants you to imagine that the pencil is a snake. At this point you start wondering if you're in the right class as you realize that this teacher has obviously given up mental health for Lent.

But, to appease him, you concentrate on the pencil being a snake. The room quiets down as you really concentrate on the word *snake*. The short little teacher starts saying things like "the snake is getting closer to you, you better watch out."

All of a sudden, just when you're in your deepest trance, you see a chair fly across the room and land on top of the snake (i.e., pencil). As the chair reaches the pencil, the teacher's voice yells out, "KILL IT!" You practically leap out of your seat. Soon you realize that the little fellow teaching the class was responsible for the chair being hurled at the pencil. It's at this point that you probably start to wonder why you paid for the course, and exactly what kind of fruitcake this guy is. Of course you're not alone, because the other students probably are thinking the same thing.

Chances are that you were in one of my commercial acting classes and the short, twirpy, fruitcake teacher was I. The point of the exercise is to see exactly where each student's "head is at" when it comes to his ideas about acting.

I then ask the class how they saw the pencil. I give them three categories to choose from. They saw it:

1. only as a pencil.
2. as a snake, but knew in the back of their minds that it was a pencil.
3. only as a snake.

At this time, I start at one side of the room asking each student to report what category he falls into. The results are very predictable from class to class. They invariably will go something like this: A few students will meekly confess to seeing it only as a pencil—category One; a few others will admit to seeing it as a snake and a pencil—category Two; and about ninety percent of the class will proudly admit to seeing it only as a snake—category Three.

The Ones usually feel out of place. They realize that if they don't have the imagination to see a pencil as a snake, it will be even harder for them to obtain the imagination needed for acting. The Twos also feel out of place. After all, they feel as though they have only "half an imagination." They think they *should* have fallen into category Three. The Twos usually look at the Ones and both groups begin to wonder if acting is really for them.

This brings us to the Threes. They feel right at home. Their eyes and faces light up like candles, as they believe they are admitting they have super imaginative powers and are therefore in the right class.

After each one has said which category he falls into, I ask the class which category they *think they should fall into.* Few, if any, ever pick category One. Obviously, if a person can't concentrate hard enough to see a pencil as a snake, he would probably have an even harder time trying to make characters come alive on the stage or screen.

A few students will say they think they should fall into category Two, but the Threes usually smirk to themselves because they think they're exactly where they should be. But are they?

In my opinion, most good actors would not fall into category Three. Oh, I'm going against all of your basic acting beliefs, am I? Sorry, but let me make my point with an example. Suppose you're on stage and at a particular moment you have to have a violent fight with another actor. If you were in the Three category, try to imagine what would happen on the stage. You'd really be fighting the other actor and this would cause obvious problems! You'd just start rambling off dialogue which didn't even appear in the script and your co-star, provided he's still with us (alive), wouldn't be able to follow your direction or dialogue. Where does this leave the other actors?

The people who run the lights, sound, and other backstage jobs take their cues from the actors' lines. What if you were so caught up in what you were doing that you "dropped" the lines which contained their cues? Suppose a stage show was a comedy and you didn't "hold" for laughs? Where would this leave the audience?

By the same token, in the screen world, you'd miss your "marks" (i.e., markers on the floor which mark your positions, discussed later) and as a result you could be out of the frame of the picture. Great, you'd be believable because you'd really be so "into" the character, but, unfortunately, no one would see your performance because you'd be out of the frame. Also, you might forget where the camera was, and therefore fail to "cheat" (discussed later) towards it when you were supposed to. Not to mention that you probably wouldn't be conscious of the "hot" of the lights (i.e., brightest spot) when the director told you to hit the "hot," because you were so wrapped up in the character. Wonderful, you'd be believable, but no one would see your performance because you'd be in the dark! I think you can see my point. Category Three is not the ideal.

This isn't to say that you shouldn't be concentrating on your character and believing in what you're doing. But at the same time, your subconscious should be saying "Move towards the camera, walk four steps to the front of the stage (no further or I might end up in the orchestra pit)," etc. Of course this inner voice is *way in the back of your mind* and should not be in the forefront, which brings us to category Two.

The category Two actor is one who concentrates on his character very hard, but who way in the back of his mind knows he's on stage or in front of the camera and will act accordingly. He probably won't walk into the orchestra pit, camera lenses, lights, or the like, because he is cognizant of where he is and what he is doing. He is a responsible actor who is where he is supposed to be, when he is supposed to be there. And, on an equally important note, this actor will believe in what he's doing, because of his strict concentration on his character. This concentration will be much more prevalent in his mind than will the concentration on the mechanics.

When you think about it, doesn't this just make good sense? I know it sounds philosophical and mysterious to say you were completely "lost in the character," but that approach really doesn't serve the best interests of your fellow actors, the stage crew, or the audience.

Frame of Reference

I hear actors say they "become" the character they're portraying. Hogwash! You can't "become" another person. No matter how hard you try, you're still going to react in certain personal ways regardless of the character you're portraying. Let's just face facts, there is no way you can have all the same exact feelings as another human being. It's impossible for you to have the same "frame of reference" as another individual. You just haven't experienced the same life as someone else. You're seeing the character through *your* eyes. And you will not interpret him the same way another actor would. If everyone did have the same frame of reference, then everyone who played Hamlet, for example, would play the character exactly the same way. But we all see Hamlet from our own perspective.

Let's take, for another example, a character who is going through a divorce. You're playing this character who at one point in the show says the line "This is going to be a dirty divorce." Everyone will think of the line differently, depending on his own experiences with divorce. You might read it one way if you yourself are actually going through a *dirty* divorce, and differently if you are going through a *friendly* one, another way if you have never been married, and maybe still another way depending on whether your parents are divorced or not. You see all the variables? Your situation will determine *to some extent* how you interpret that line. There is actually no way to take away your own personal interpretation, and really no one should want to. That's what makes your portrayal of a character unique and different from that of the other actors who might play the same role. This is not to say that one interpretation is better or worse than the next. It is only to say that they are different. (It *is* true, of course, that some interpretations might be more interesting than others.) These variations are what give our characters "character."

But how might you give a successful interpretation to a role for which your personal experience has not prepared you? You can expand your frame of reference *beyond* your own experience. You learn to do this through *observation*—one of the greatest continuing "studies" you can do for the acting profession.

Observation

On a particular day your agent sends you to an interview for the part of a doctor. Although you might have a few acquaintances who are doctors, let's suppose you don't really know the tensions, the worries, the decisions, and the condominium problems with which a doctor must contend. You are in a panic about how to portray a character about whom you have no understanding.

The next day, your agent sends you to an interview for the part of an Arctic explorer. You are still trying to recover from the day before when you had to play a doctor. What diverse characters! The screen test takes place in a soundstage at Universal Studios, where it's so hot under the lights that when you get up from your chair to be interviewed, the chair follows you. But you must act cold just the same. Do you know how to act cold? Do you know how people look, feel, and react under such circumstances? Do you even know how *you* react to hot and cold temperatures? Maybe not.

But as an actor you are going to play all kinds of roles. You might not have the time to study your character before shooting on a particular acting job, and you might not have any time even to think about the character before an interview, especially in the commercial field. In fact, you might not know what type of character you're going to audition for before you actually get there! This is the rule, rather than the exception in commercial acting. So you must be prepared ahead to interview for a variety of characters.

There is no way to learn something about all types of people, but one tool that will help you to understand people, to improve your interpretation, is OBSERVATION. Commercial actors are usually placed in environments which are typical to the average person. They may not speak dialogue that is typical (who runs around the house talking about how great their feminine deodorant is?), but the occupations and situations are usually fairly normal. Most actors realize the importance of watching other actors perform. Watching other actors is very important, but many actors tend to forget that actors are interpreting roles. So watch performances, but also GET TO THE SOURCE—watch people in real-life situations.

So the next time you are in a doctor's office, *observe* the way the doctor acts, reacts, studies, and feels. Watch the precision with which he makes his diagnosis. Notice the way he takes down information about you. Really listen to what he says and really pay attention to his reactions and expressions.

The same applies to the role of the Arctic explorer. No, you might not see such people every day, but you can observe the way people react when they are cold. Even if you live in a warm climate, you can still watch "cold" reactions. The TV news, TV entertainment and commercials, magazine pictures, etc., are among the many ways to observe people in different situations. You can watch what they do with their hands, legs, and faces when they are cold. For instance, they may wrap their arms around their bodies, rub their hands together, shiver, and shift about restlessly. You know that people do all of these things because you have observed them. And, very importantly, you probably have noticed yourself doing these very same things. Of course, all people in cold weather do not react the same way, but you might find some commonalities in their reactions. You can store these as well as some of the uncommon reactions which might be useful, in your "memory bank" for future reference.

But, when playing a doctor, for example, be careful not to clump *all* doctors together using a stereotype. The doctor you play has specific traits, and drawing on the general ideas that you get from real doctors, you will be better able to form those *specifics*. You will find that some people in the same profession share some characteristics. (For instance, all doctors write your prescriptions illegibly and always write your bills clearly.)

Also, observe everyday people in terms of their emotional types. For example, shy people and outgoing people do not have the same mannerisms. They walk differently, speak differently, sit differently, even eat differently. Their expressions of emotions such as happiness, sadness, anger, and fear will be varied. And don't forget to make note of cultural and regional disparities. A New Yorker may show pride, embarrassment, or surprise in a different way than will a Texan, for example.

You will want to observe commercials in order to familiarize yourself with the various approaches of the different companies. First of all, as far as physical type is concerned, it is a grave misconception that only beautiful people have a chance at commercial acting. In fact, this couldn't be further from the truth. Commercial advertisers will often use everyday-looking people so that the public can identify with them. In general, the "look" that sponsors want will depend upon both the product they are selling and the image they are trying to project. A company that sells beer probably will want an actor who appears tough and rugged, while one that produces wine might prefer someone who looks more refined and sophisticated. Similarly, a person who wears Orson Wells designer jeans might not be welcome in an ad for Diet Pepsi.

Dress, too, is important in commercial advertising. Keep in mind here, as before, the overall image and tone of the commercials you watch. In a cologne ad, an actor in a sweat suit would find it difficult to relay sophistication to his audience. By the same token, women in evening gowns are rarely, if ever, seen in the faster-paced, family-oriented fast-food commercials. Humor, of course, is much more flexible. Anyone from women in tennis dresses to men in tuxedos can be funny.

In fact, you'll see that clearly if you start watching people—and yourself! Comedy comes from real life. I've noticed that whenever I'm at the airport standing in a line and I want to go to the bathroom, I'll ask some perfect stranger to watch my bags, so that some other perfect stranger won't steal them. Now to me, that's funny. And, for another example, I've always wondered why they put "Wanted" posters in the Post Office . . . what do they want me to do, write the guy? How come they didn't hold the sucker when they took his picture? Speaking of law, I've always wondered why they lock up the jury and let the defendant go free . . . . I could go on and on, but the point is clear: You can learn so much about the elements of comedy by observation.

All the kinds of observation discussed here can help you in your approach to commercial interviews. Now, when you interview for, let's say, a suntan lotion commercial, you will have a better idea of what physical and emotional type of person will be needed, how he should be dressed, and what kind of overall image he should present. So start preparing yourself for the commercial acting profession right this minute. Start observing!

Memory Substitution

Suppose you get an acting role in which you have to yell at some person in the scene. This person has been treating you very badly (in the script) for the past six months and you have to give him a piece of your mind. And let's suppose you are a female and you're cast in the above scene. You must yell at this guy who is playing opposite you. You arrive on the set early to meet your partner. Actually, after talking with him for a few minutes you think the guy is such a "hunk" that he could make a stone pass out. You really don't feel like yelling at him, but that's what the scene calls for.

Or, let's say you are a male cast in a romantic role and you personally don't like the female the producers have cast to play your girl friend. She's just not your type. In real life you have a Ph.D. in quantum physics and she's the type who takes the phone off the hook to watch the "Dukes of Hazzard."

The point is clear: Actors often have to be in situations that don't conform with their personal lives (or likes). As a matter of fact, because scenes are shot out of sequence (to be discussed in detail in Chapter 2), you might be in situations that are emotional opposites of each other *during the same day*. In the morning you might shoot a scene where you're very happy, and in the afternoon shoot one where you have to be very sad, and so on. If you aren't convincing in each scene, then the whole production falls flat.

In acting, we use something called SUBSTITUTION. We substitute something imagined from our memory for the current situation. Let's take the first example above—the female who has to yell at a man in one particular scene. You have never met the person, yet you have to tell him how horribly he's been treating you for the past six months. To make matters worse, in real life when you look at him, you have a meltdown. You must substitute something in your mind for the situation at hand. Perhaps you could concentrate on a guy whom you personally can't stand. You would like to wrap a pound of hamburger around that guy's neck and let him play with the neighbor's German shepherd. So concentrate on the person you dislike and carry those feelings over to the person you're playing opposite. The anger, meanness, and hatred will come through.

And in the second example, let's suppose you're the male lead and you have to tell your female co-star how much you love her and then give her a kiss that would cost three dollars in a taxi— on camera for millions of people to see. You love intelligent people and she's the type whose brain scan would be a still life. Again, you can substitute with the feeling for someone that you really do love at that particular time in real life. It all sounds easy enough, but it takes a lot of concentration to pull it off. The actor has to accept it first, then the audience will follow suit.

There are some critics of the above idea, who say that an actor should not have to "substitute" for anything. These critics say that the actor should be "on his toes" enough to "grab the moment" and be able to relate to the scene no matter what takes place in it. If an actor can do that every time, more power to him. But there are going to be scenes where you can't directly relate. And there are going to be times when the props you'll use are nothing like the real thing (for an example, see Chapter 5). SUBSTITUTION may be necessary to get you through it all. In fact, it is the basis of acting, in my opinion.

Chapter Two

Terminology and Procedure

There are basically three types of commercials: Spokesman, Slice-of-Life, and Voice-Over Narrative.

The Spokesman commercial consists of someone talking directly to the camera selling a certain product. This person represents the sponsor. There are many examples of famous actors in spokesman commercials, among them Michael Landon for Kodak, Karl Malden for American Express, and Jaclyn Smith for Wella Balsam. But this doesn't leave you out. The stars actually compose only a small percentage of the spokesmen used in the commercial industry.

The Slice-of-Life commercial consists of a short story which usually contains a beginning, a middle, and an end. These commercials are the ones you see where everything is resolved at the end because the people used a particular product. For example, the story might consist of a husband and wife who are having problems in their marriage because the husband doesn't like his wife's coffee. But, Mrs. Olson saves the marriage at the end of the commercial because she comes to the rescue with Folger's.

The Voice-Over Narrative commercial consists of an actor who is on camera who talks to a voice which is off camera. An example would be a housewife who is looking into the mirror thinking how horrible she looks. Out of nowhere a voice tells her what brand of shampoo to use. She uses the product, thanks the voice, and everyone lives happily ever after.

All of the above commercials basically fall into two categories: the Hard Sell and the Soft Sell.

The *Hard Sell* aggressively urges that you purchase the product or service immediately (or else!).

The *Soft Sell* demonstrates the advantage of the product or service without specifically demanding that you buy it.

Script Terms

It's extremely important that the actor who is interviewing for a commercial know exactly what is happening visually in that commercial. This knowledge will give him clues as to how broad (big) he can play the character physically and emotionally. For instance, if the camera is very tight (close-up) on your face, then you can't make as big a movement with your body and face, as you could if the camera were farther away. Movement on a close shot has to be restricted or you could easily go right off the screen.

Too many actors brush over this important aspect of studying the script. It's a good idea to read the *video* section (meaning visual action; usually found on the left side of the page) first to get an overview of the entire commercial. Then read the *audio* section (containing all sound aspects of the commercial; usually found on the right side of the page) to work on the dialogue. Not all commercial scripts you see on the interviews will contain the video (the "shooting script" isn't always available to the actor on the interview), but if it does contain the information, take advantage of it.

The following list of definitions should provide you with a basic understanding of the terms that are used in the average commercial.

SHOT: what is recorded by a single operation of the camera from the time it starts to the time it stops.

TAKE: a single attempt to record a shot on camera. During the taping of a commercial there will be many takes of a particular shot.

Types of Shots

ECU: Extreme Close-Up—a shot in which the camera is focused very close to its subject. This type of shot, for example, could be of a person's nose, mouth, hand, or foot. It could also be of the product or product name. If the ECU is on any part of the actor, he must remain very still to remain in the frame.

CU: Close-Up—a shot which is farther from the subject than the Extreme Close-Up, but closer than the Medium Close-Up. An example would be a close shot of an actor's face.

MCU: Medium Close-Up—a shot which is farther from the subject than the Close-Up, but closer than the Medium Shot. An example would be a shot of a person's head and shoulders or a shot from the bust line up.

MS: Medium Shot—a shot taken at a greater distance from the subject than the MCU but less than the Long Shot. A Medium Shot of a person would cover the area from the waist up.

LS: Long Shot—a shot taken at a considerable distance from the subject. It could show a whole room or an actor's entire body.

GROUP SHOT: a shot containing three or more people, or products.

HIGH ANGLE SHOT: a shot taken from higher than normal eye level down on the actor or product.

LOOSE SHOT: a shot which isn't very close to its subject(s). This usually refers to a Medium Shot (MS) or a Long Shot (LS).

LOW ANGLE SHOT: a shot taken from below normal eye level up at the actor or product.

MASTER SHOT: a wide shot which usually shows all the principal actors in a scene.

OVER-THE-SHOULDER SHOT: a shot taken from the perspective of over an actor's shoulders.

POV: Point-of-View—a shot approximating the perspective of an actor.

SINGLE SHOT: a shot which contains only one person or product.

TIGHT SHOT: a shot which is very close to its subject. This usually refers to an Extreme Close-Up (ECU) or a Close-Up (CU).

TWO SHOT: a shot which contains two actors or products.

WIDE SHOT: a shot covering a relatively large area of the set. This usually refers to a Long Shot (LS).

Other Script Terms

BG: Background—the area of the shot which is behind the main action. An example in the script would be: "IN THE BG THERE IS A CROWD OF COLLEGE STUDENTS."

CUT: the joining of two separate shots so that the first is *instantaneously* replaced by the second. When said on the set, however, "cut" means to stop the action.

DISSOLVE: a scene transition whereby one shot *gradually* replaces another shot.

EXT: Exterior—a shot that is taken outdoors. An example in the script would be: "EXT. JIM'S HOUSE."

FADE: the process whereby the image on screen gradually goes from light to dark, or vice versa. This type of transition usually takes place at the end of a commercial.

HERO: the actual product (hamburger, soft drink can, car, etc.) used in a particular scene. For example, if McDonald's is shooting a "Big Mac" commercial, the actual hamburger used in each take is chosen from many such burgers. That chosen one is called the "hero."

INT: Interior—a shot that is taken indoors. An example in the script would be: "INT. JILL'S BEDROOM."

MOS: Mit-Out Sound—a shot taken without sound. An example in the script would be: "WOMAN WASHING KITCHEN COUNTER (MOS)."

O.C.: On Camera—anything (usually action) which is recorded by the camera during a shot. An example in the script would be: "LS OF TONY AS BILL SLAMS DOOR IN THE BG (O.C.)."

OPENING: the first shot of the commercial.

O.S.: Off Screen—actions or sounds related to the commercial that are not recorded by the camera during a shot. An example in the script would be: "CU OF TONY AS WE HEAR BILL SLAMMING DOOR IN THE BG (O.S.)."

SFX: Special Effects—graphics or sounds normally added after the actual shooting of the commercial.

SUPER: Superimposition—one image appears over another (much like a double exposure). In commercial work, the term usually refers to words displayed over the recorded images. An example in the script would be: "SUPER: 'COKE ADDS LIFE.'"

VO: Voice-Over—words spoken off camera which accompany the images on screen. In other words, the actor speaking is off camera.

The Storyboard

The script may be in the form of a storyboard. The storyboard is a drawing of what each shot will look like, much like a cartoon or comic strip. Under each picture are written the words that accompany the image. The storyboard isn't always available for the actor on every commercial interview, but if you are lucky enough to see it, study it carefully. It will give you the most accurate picture of what type of image the interviewers are looking for.

The Storyboard (actual size of each board: 25″ × 19″)

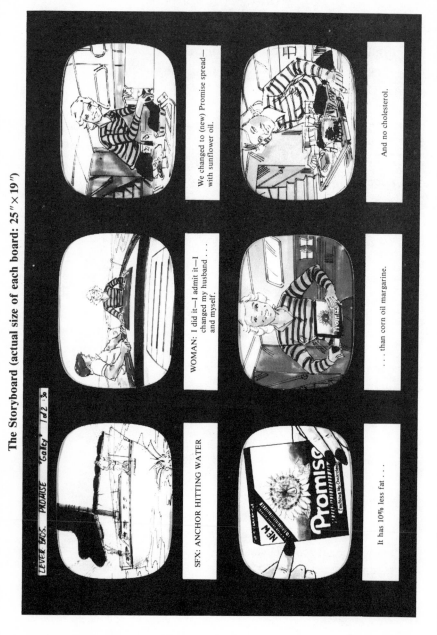

LEVER BROS.   PROMISE   "Galey"   1 of 2 :30

We changed to (new) Promise spread— with sunflower oil.

And no cholesterol.

WOMAN: I did it—I admit it—I changed my husband . . . and myself.

. . . than corn oil margarine.

SFX: ANCHOR HITTING WATER

It has 10% less fat . . .

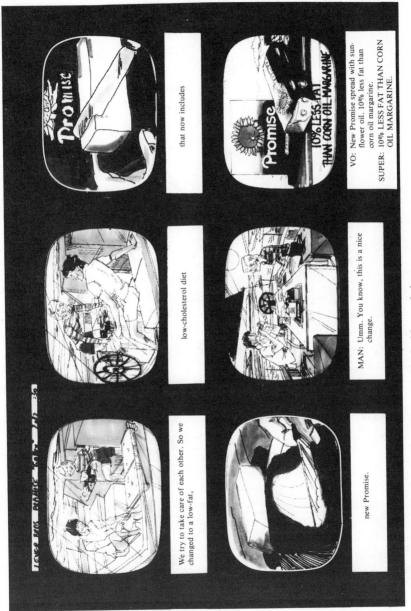

that now includes

low-cholesterol diet

LEVER BRO PROMO 60 1 222 88

We try to take care of each other. So we changed to a low-fat,

VO: New Promise spread with sun-flower oil. 10% less fat than corn oil margarine.
SUPER: 10% LESS FAT THAN CORN OIL MARGARINE.

MAN: Umm. You know, this is a nice change.

new Promise.

How a Commercial Is Shot

"Golly Gee, Mom, my teeth have stains on them."
"Golly Gee, Son, I see what you mean."
"Golly, Mom, what can I do about the stains?"
"Gee, Son, try using Presto 98 Teeth Cleaner."
"Gee, Mom, you're the greatest."
"Gee, Son, so is Presto 98 Teeth Cleaner."

The above sample commercial script seems like a fairly simple commercial to shoot. There are only six lines and one would assume that the actors in the above commercial would just stand next to each other and shoot the lines. You might think that such a commercial could be shot in under fifteen minutes, tops. WRONG!! Those lines could take an entire day, and some commercials even take longer.

Why should such a fuss be made over these few lines? In a stage play, for example, a few lines go by so quickly that one can hardly remember them at the end of the play. But, the few lines in the above commercial are the entire "show."

On stage there is continuity. That is to say, the play will begin at the beginning and continue without interruption (except for intermissions) until the end of the play. The play has a natural progression of events and each scene will be executed only once every performance.

The same is not true for TV, film, and commercials. Shootings are not done in the actual sequence that appears in the final product, and there will be many "cuts" between scenes.

For instance, in the above commercial, let's suppose that the first two lines take place in the living room, the next two in the bathroom, and the last two back in the living room. If we shot the commercial in the order in which it is written, the film crew would have to set up the first shot in the living room. Then they would have to move everything—camera, lights, etc.—from the living room to the bathroom for the second scene. Once that was completed, they would have to spend another four or five hours setting up the final shot back in the living room.

As you can see, this would be very time consuming. There is, however, a way to reduce all this moving around. What if we shot both the first and last scene in the living room while we were there, instead of coming back to the same setup? That would save many, many hours, wouldn't it?

What you as the actor must understand is that with this gain in efficiency comes a loss in continuity. For example, suppose a certain commercial involves your walking up to a house, opening the front door, and talking with another actor in the living room. The scene may flow very nicely in the final commercial, but in the actual shooting a production company could use a completely different house (or the studio) for the interior shots. Those two shots might not even be done on the same day. Trying to "match" scenes can become an enormous problem in commercials (and magnify that for the shooting of a movie!).

Even the individual scene itself has constant "cuts." For instance, first the production company will shoot what is called the "master shot." This is an *establishing shot* to show who is in the scene. We shoot the first scene of the commercial—the one in the living room. We show both Mom and Son speaking their lines. We've now shown the audience who is in the scene and set the foundation for the action following.

Now we'll move in for the close-ups. First, we will shoot Mom's. This shot is from the son's POV (point of view); the camera will be only on Mom and we will not see the son at all during these takes. Sometimes, depending on the angle, the actor Mom is talking to might be able to stand in his original position, but this is the exception. In many cases, the person being talked to for these takes cannot be in his original position because the camera will be there. The son will have to stand off camera, and Mom will have to look towards his original direction—where the camera is now.

Next we'll shoot Son's close-ups. The shot is reversed, with the mom being over to one side and the camera being on Son (i.e., the shot is from Mom's POV). Again, these shots take hours to set up. Every time there is a change—for example, a camera moving to a different position—the whole set has to be relit, etc. (And you will find that it can be very disconcerting to direct your conversation in one direction when the person with whom you are talking is in another, even for a few lines. PRACTICE!)

Next we'll shoot the "over-the-shoulder" shots. First we'll shoot Mom's. In other words, the son will stand in his original position, while the camera, which is behind him, will be focused on Mom. We again run through the same two lines. Then we'll reverse the over-the-shoulder shot and focus in on the son. Mom will stand in her original position, while we shoot over her shoulders, filming the son and his reactions. The actors, again, run through the same two lines.

That basically takes care of those first two lines. Of course there are many other shots which can be used. We can, for example, shoot a "low" and "high" angle on Mom and Son, respectively. In other words we might shoot up at the mom, and down at the son. This could perhaps give Mom the superiority—she's the one handling the product! Shooting up at someone tends to give him the advantage, and shooting down at someone tends to put him in an inferior position. When you're watching TV notice the angles. For instance, a husband and wife might be having an argument. Even though the husband may be taller than the wife, the director might decide to shoot down at the husband and up at the wife. This gives the audience the impression that perhaps the wife is psychologically winning this argument. You should watch the way commercials are put together as they unfold on TV—this awareness will help your performance. Remember all I told you earlier about *observation*.

The point is, shooting a commercial can be a long, grueling day. I've only given you a thumbnail sketch of how the shooting takes place. Remember that each setup (i.e., different shot) takes many hours to arrange. The commercial may even be shot with many different variations and scripts. This means all of the above steps would probably be repeated for each script. BE PREPARED FOR HARD WORK WHEN SHOOTING A COMMERCIAL.

Then, all those hours of work and roles of film will be edited into a final product(s) to be shown to various audiences for testing. And, after all the testing has been completed it might possibly be re-edited again and again before being shown to the general public.

As you read the next few chapters keep in mind the commercial shooting illustration in this chapter. When you are preparing for dialogue delivery and performance of physical movements, it's important that you realize the obstacles you'll be performing under when actually shooting a commercial.

Chapter Three

Commercial Dialogue

This chapter deals with general concepts concerning commercial dialogue. The information tends to apply to the commercial interview more than the actual shooting (though there's much overlap), because when you're actually shooting a commercial, the director will have many of his own ideas and concepts about the dialogue. The general rules that follow will, however, be extremely helpful to you with dialogue interpretation which will aid you in winning commercial roles.

Many products advertised on TV are not in themselves exciting or even mildly interesting. The ad agency is in charge of the script, but it's your responsibility as an actor to present the product in a unique and interesting way. Even the most common, mundane article can be transformed into an appealing product. What would toilet paper be without Mr. Whipple?

One important concept I hope you learn is that it's not only *what* you *say,* but *how* you *say* it. For example, the phrase "Excuse me," really isn't that funny. But when Steve Martin says, "EXCUUUUUUUUSE ME," he gets a gigantic laugh. Words in and of themselves, as with lines, generally aren't what gets the laugh or meaning across. The same is true with commercials. The actor, by his interpretation of the dialogue, will, or will not, get the message across to the public.

An interesting exercise which I sometimes employ in class shows how an effective actor can say a line that means nothing and make it mean something. I tell two students to go outside of the classroom and discuss a scene they'd like to show to the class. They discuss where they're going to be, whom they're going to play, what their relationship to each other will be, etc. They then come back into the room. I give them two phone books to use as scripts. In other words, they have to read directly from the phone book, but put in all of the inflections, pauses, etc., that they would put in were they saying actual lines of a script. If the two do a good job, the audience is able to discover what is going on in the scene. The point is, the two actors are getting their message across to the audience purely through their delivery. Their interpretation of the lines is more important than the actual lines of the "script."

Actors interpreting lines can fall into either of two obvious traps: overplaying and underplaying. Putting too much emphasis on the words has the same effect as reading a book with every word in it capitalized or italicized; since everything stands out, nothing does. Hit every word and it's a sure bet that the message will become lost. What makes something stand out is its difference from the other parts of the script.

While trying to avoid overplaying, many actors tend to put too *little* emphasis in their interpretation. Their performance then becomes lackluster—*dull.* And that certainly is not going to sell anything! Commercial acting takes a lot of energy. The usual rule of thumb in commercial acting is: MAKE IT BIG because the director can always pull you down, while it is much harder for him to get more out of you. (A word must be said here about the difference in TV and film acting from commercial acting. In TV [with the exception of situation comedies] and film acting, "less is more"; you want to underplay, not overplay.)

The sections below will explain the major points you need to learn, so that your interpretation will be the most effective. The divisions I have chosen will help you to review the major elements individually. Just remember that they do overlap and relate to one another, and that you will want to work on each as a part of the *whole.*

Reading

It's interesting that people think an actor should "read" his lines. Ironically, that's exactly what you *don't* want from the actor. For example, when you're talking to someone on the phone, it's very easy for the other person to distinguish your *reading* to him as opposed to *talking* to him. Similarly, when someone gives a speech, it's easy to tell when he's reading rather than being conversational. YOU ARE A HUMAN BEING TALKING, AND YOU SHOULD SOUND LIKE A HUMAN BEING TALKING!

Though the script you perform for a commercial probably isn't written in your own words, it should sound like your own words. This is the trick to any form of acting; commercials are certainly no different in this department. The public should believe that you are just telling them, in your own words, how great the product is. The minute the viewing public realizes you are reading from a script prepared by some Madison Avenue ad executive, is the minute you, and the product, lose credibility.

After you have learned a script, be careful that you don't "see it" in your mind. I can't tell you how many times I've seen actors' eyes just slightly moving from side to side as the actors recite dialogue—which is the tip-off that they're actually "seeing" and "reading" the script in their minds. I sometimes can actually see their eyes "end" on one line and drop down to the next line in the left hand margin to begin a new sentence. Forget where the lines are on the page. You should "say" the words as though they just came to you from your own mind, even though they are really from the script.

When you're "saying" the lines, forget those old reading inflections you used in high school when reading aloud. Forget conventional rhythmic reading habits that we have all learned. We don't talk that way! Everyday conversation is quite different from regular reading. There's a different attitude in regular conversation as opposed to reading; talking is friendlier. Reading tends to become stilted and cold.

Also, reading the lines makes the script sound too perfect; people don't talk perfectly. The tendency for amateur actors is to read all the lines smoothly and easily. But in real life, people stutter, pause, hesitate on certain words, speed up in the middle of a sentence, make weird sounds in between words and thoughts, run sentences together, etc. They do just about everything *but* speak their "lines" smoothly and easily.

While hesitating on words, pausing for effect, changing rhythm and pace, etc., keep in mind that your performance shouldn't sound sloppy. There's a big difference between "natural" dialogue and "sloppy" dialogue. Your speech must be uneven enough to make it sound natural, but no so unbalanced that it sounds unprofessional. If you become so sloppy that you sound like a fool and can't be understood, that's just as bad as being so perfect that no one believes what you're saying.

While you're tailoring your dialogue for a natural effect, be careful not to change the wording of the script. When you're actually shooting a commercial, you'll have to follow the script exactly word-for-word for legal reasons. In the interview a few words changed here or there because you don't know it perfectly won't make that much difference, but you should still stick as closely to the script as you can. Remember, some ad executive spent many hours on that script and it was approved by both the agency and the client before it got to you.

Analyzing the Script

It's very important for an actor to understand what he is saying in a commercial. How can you interpret dialogue from a play, for example, if you don't know what meaning the character is supposed to get across? The same is true with commercials. You should examine the script closely enough to fully understand the overall purpose, or message, and the meaning of each sentence as it fits into that purpose.

At the same time, be careful not to analyze the script to death on the interview. Once you've decided how you are going to get the meaning across using the sentences mentioning the product (see Chapter 5 for details), I'd avoid trying to figure out which words to emphasize in every sentence—or you could lose the natural flavor of the script.

Let's take the sentence "I'm going to the park." It seems like a simple enough sentence with a direct meaning. If you change the emphasis from one word to another, however, the sentence takes on new meanings. For example:

"I'M going to the park." This means that I am going and not you or anyone else.

"I'm GOING to the park." This means that you aren't going to stop me; I'm going anyway, no matter what you say or think.

"I'm going to the PARK." This means that I'm going to the park and not anywhere else.

You can see from the above demonstration that you can take a sentence, change the emphasis from one word to the next, and you have a new sentence with a whole new meaning. The way to handle this in a commercial, basically, is just to say the words while keeping in your mind the meaning behind what you're saying. (See the exercise described in the section on "Coloring Words," later in this chapter.) You do this in real life. You don't think to yourself, "Now I'm going to tell him that I'm going to the park and the emphasis should be on the word *going*." No, you're concentrating on the fact that you are going to tell him you're going to the park and that neither he nor anyone else is going to stop you. And when you say that sentence you'll say it with the right emphasis— "I'm GOING to the park." It will become stilted if you concentrate solely on the words to emphasize instead of the meaning of what you're trying to get across to the other person.

A note on marking the script: When an actor gets the commercial script, I think it's a bad idea to underline words and mark the script, but this is strictly a personal belief. For me, if I try to follow the marks on a page, my delivery of the commercial dialogue sounds very rehearsed and phony. It might be right for *you* to mark the script, but be careful that you don't think you have to follow those marks each time you rehearse it. If you do, then you're going to fall into rhythmic patterns which we talked about earlier. In everyday life we don't say the same sentences the same way each time we use them—even if the situation is somewhat the same. We let the words flow freely. This is the natural quality that advertisers look for in commercial actors.

Coloring Words

You want to "color" the words when saying commercial dialogue. You want to make a word sound like what it says. Particularly, look for adjectives in the script. Actually, you color words when you speak in everyday conversation. For example, you say "WOW, it was FANTASTIC." The *wow* and *fantastic* sound exciting. We express emotion more freely in everyday conversation than we do when we're reading.

Suppose you were to say, "It's real soft," reading from the script. You might not say the word *soft* any more softly than you say the other words; the color might be missing from the word *soft*. Once again, we get back to the importance of *observation* for the actor. Watch for the color in everyone's speech. You'll be amazed at how people will make words sound like what they mean.

If you are having a hard time coloring words and making a script sound natural, here is a suggestion to help you accomplish the task. After you have read over the commercial a few times, put the script aside while you think about the full meaning behind the lines without concentrating on each specific word in the script. Try to come up with an image (or set of images) that represents your personal interpretation of the message. Now pick up the script and say those lines of commercial dialogue, keeping that picture in mind, or put the script down and make up your own words to get across the same message. You'll notice a change in your speech. The "color" of the image will naturally show up in the appropriate word or words. Now, this is the way the commercial should sound.

Transitions

By concentrating on the meaning of what you're saying as opposed to individual words, you'll observe transitions. We group together words and ideas that belong together. Our voice and attitude automatically change when we move from one thought to the next. That thought change can come at the end of a sentence or in the middle of one.

An example of a typical transition might be: "Susie, you're so sweet. Thanks so much for the present. Oh, did you get mine?" You can see the obvious change of attitude (i.e., transition) from "Thanks so much for the present" to "Oh, did you get mine?"

Transitions occur constantly in everyone's speech, so look for them. Be sure to use them when reading commercial dialogue so that your delivery will appear natural.

Pacing the Copy

Though you should have high energy while saying the dialogue, DON'T RUSH THE COPY. Actors tend to get nervous and run through the copy entirely too rapidly. You can probably remember in high school giving a speech that was supposed to be, for example, five minutes in length. You practiced at home and it came out to five minutes and ten seconds, another time five minutes and three seconds, and so on. Perhaps when you got up in front of the class, however, it came out to about three minutes because you were speaking at 150 words-per-minute with gusts up to 190.

We must give the audience time to let our message sink into their brains. The nervous actor tends to run words and sentences together, not giving the audience time to digest what has been said. The performance looks phony because the performer isn't taking the time to collect his thoughts; people usually take the time to think of what they're going to say next.

Pauses not only make it appear as though you are collecting you own thoughts, but they also give the audience time to digest theirs and yours. This is definitely not to say that you should putt-putt along. You don't want the commercial message to "drag." Usually, something drags when there are gaps in the reading. There is a distinct difference between a gap and a pause. A gap is a break in the character, meaning that the actor has stopped the thinking and feeling process for some reason other than the right one. When someone pauses in natural conversation, he is still thinking and feeling what he is saying.

As time progresses, you'll get the idea of how fast or slow the script should be delivered. It all gets back to OBSERVATION. Watch commercials to get an idea how quickly or slowly the actors in them say the dialogue.

Speaking From the Script or Q-Cards

In the actual shooting of a commercial, obviously you won't be allowed to read from a script, and rarely will Q-cards be used, because you will have had some time to learn your lines. But during most commercial interviews you will be permitted to speak your lines from a copy of the script, or less frequently, you will say them from Q-cards. For one thing, you will have had only a short time to look over the script. For another, the producers are usually in such a hurry when it comes to casting a commercial that they don't have time to give you the script to take home and memorize. Besides, if they did do that they'd have to pay you a small fee (if the commercial is being shot under union jurisdiction).

If you are interviewing for the commercial solo, you probably will be asked to deliver your lines to the camera. Therefore, your attention must be divided between the script and camera, or Q-card and camera, depending on the particular interview. Naturally, the more you look at the camera (i.e., public's eyes), the more sincere you seem to be. This is why you should arrive at the interview early so that you'll have a chance to become familiar with the script.

Below are tips on how to read from scripts and Q-cards at commercial interviews. You should read Chapter 9 of this book for other guidelines for working with the script and Q-cards at the interview, and Chapter 4 for more details on movement of the head and eyes in general.

Speaking from the Script

There are two things you need to watch out for when reading from the script: (1) holding it too high, and (2) holding it too low.

If you hold the script too high, you will cover your face—a no-no. The script should not be above your chin. Actors tend to think that because they can see over the script their faces are not hidden. Your eyes are much higher up on your face than is your chin, so the fact that you can see over the script does not necessarily mean your complete face is in view.

If you hold the script too low, you create the "bobbing for apples" effect. You have to hold your head down to read the script if it's too low; then you have to bring your head back up to say a few lines; and then you have to drop it back again to read from the script. Also, this vertical movement of the head takes a moment, leaving you less time to be looking into the camera lens (i.e., the public's eyes) or at the person to whom you are speaking in the commercial. Sometimes when the "bobbing head" becomes extreme, your face can actually drop completely out of the frame of the camera. And, even if it doesn't go that far, your face can still fall enough to where the audience only sees the top of your head—not a pretty picture! (Keep in mind that some of the people responsible for casting will be seeing you on the videotape, not in person at the interview.)

The best policy is to hold the script just below the chin. This way your head can stay stationary when you're looking down at it. Basically, only your eyes need to look down. This short movement of your eyes from the script to camera or script to another actor will give you more time to look at whatever you are supposed to be looking at in the commercial. If you use this method, your performance will be much more pleasant to watch.

Speaking from Q-Cards

With Q-cards, you don't have to worry about the "bobbing head" problem. On the other hand, sometimes people can tell that you are reading from them because they can see your eyes and head moving back and forth to read the lines.

One way to make it appear as though you aren't reading Q-cards is to move your head slightly as you talk. But the head movement should not be horizontal long enough to make it appear as though you're reading a line. The movement should be much smaller, as though you are just gesturing with your head. (I don't mean swishing your head back and forth constantly.) The *slight* head movement will compensate for the movement of your eyes, making the eye movement much less noticeable. The idea is to really try to read *down* the Q-card rather than from side to side.

Projection

Screen actors must remember that the microphone is right above their heads. Many actors who are accustomed to working on the stage tend to project very loudly because they are used to trying to hit the back row of the theatre. When you're working on camera, however, the mike is usually an inch or two away from you. If you project as you would on stage, it will sound as though you're yelling. The audience (i.e., microphone) is too close for that sort of thing. Now this is not to say that you should whisper, *especially for a commercial.* But keep in mind that you don't have to project your voice very far.

This is also not to say that your energy level should be low; quite the contrary. Many commercials are bigger than life and they demand much more energy than would a similar real-life situation. The animation should be visible on your face.

Relating to Your Partner

When you are working with a partner, make sure your dialogue "matches" and relates to his. Unfortunately an actor sometimes falls into the trap of isolating himself from his partner. He gets set in his mind which way his own lines should be said before he hears the other person. He has been studying his lines and naturally he also has had to learn most of the lines (if not every single word) of his partner. So, though he may *hear* what the partner is saying, he may not really be *listening*.

Once upon a time I was in New York performing in a play when one of the actors made an entrance and started to recite the lines in ACT III. This would have been fine if the actor had been sober and if the rest of the cast had been in ACT III. Unfortunately, the play had just begun and we were in ACT I. Since this actor had given the plot away before I could usher him off stage ad-libbing such things as, "Time for bed, Grandpa," we were in deep trouble. The other three actors and I had another hour-and-a-half to fill, while the audience already knew the outcome.

I learned a big lesson that night. I learned the art of listening on stage. As an actor I had always been told that you have to listen carefully to what the other actors are saying even though you know everyone's lines by heart, or your reactions will be fake. That night I really had to listen and concentrate on everything the other three actors were saying so that I could ad-lib with them. Though I can't speak for the story line that night, I can say that we actors gave our most believable performance of the entire run of the show.

You and I know that in real life people "play off of each other." We react in accordance with *how* the other person speaks to us, as well as to the words he is saying. In everyday life we listen to what the other person is saying, interpret in our minds what he has said to us, and quickly decide how we're going to react to it. We listen with our eyes as well as with our ears, i.e., we watch his face, body, hands, etc.

The first step, then, in relating to your partner in a performance of any kind is *listening*. When you are relating to your partner, if actor *A* says a line to you, you'll react one way, and if actor *B* says that same exact line to you, you'll react another way—because actors *A* and *B* aren't delivering the line to you in the same manner. You must play off each other. Otherwise, we have two actors reading lines to each other giving their own separate performances without having any real conversation between them.

A good exercise here is to get another actor to work with you and pick up a script that neither you nor your partner has seen before. Have your partner read one character's line and then you make up a line to fit his line. Then have your partner read the next line for his character in the script, and so on. In other words, only your partner will read the lines from the script and you have to fill in the gaps. In this exercise, it's not important whether or not you fill in with sentences like that of the character you would be playing in the script. The essential thing here is that you listen carefully to your partner. You will really have to relate to him in order to make the scene work.

A final word of caution: Be sure not to "mimic" other actors. There's nothing more distracting than watching actor *A*'s lips moving while actor *B* is speaking. Actor *A* might be thinking of his own lines or he might be saying his partner's lines to himself following down the script. Either way, this is very distracting for the audience and especially for the partner.

* * *

You may wish to practice delivering commerical dialogue using the scripts in Appendix A of this book. Some you can practice alone; for others you will want to call in a partner. Another thing you might find helpful is to tape record some commercials that have principal roles of the same "types" you like to portray. You can transcribe those commercials from your tape recording and, with as much video reference as you wish, practice delivering the dialogue. Tape that practice for review later too.

When you listen to the commercials—both actual ones and your own practice tapes—keep in mind the various concepts discussed in this chapter. Notice, for example: Did the actor say the lines "perfectly"? If not, how did he personalize them a bit? Did the actor "color" words? How? Notice how transitions were handled. And what about pacing? And the matching of dialogue? With this exercise you are building skills and practicing that important technique of *observation,* with the concentration on sound.

Chapter Four

Basic Camera Staging

Before you interview for a commercial, as well as before you shoot one, you should know certain staging directions and techniques very well. First of all, let's review the basic stage directions, which also generally apply for camera work.

UPSTAGE is away from the audience or camera. DOWNSTAGE is towards the audience or camera and away from the back of the stage or studio. (These terms come from the English theatre where many of the stages are "raked"—starting low at the edge closest to the audience and rising gradually, to the edge farthest away from the audience.) STAGE LEFT is to the actor's left as he faces the audience or camera, not to the audience's or camera's left. STAGE RIGHT is to the actor's right, in the same fashion. CENTER STAGE is in the center of the stage or center of the camera frame. DOWNSTAGE RIGHT is towards the audience or camera and to the actor's right. DOWNSTAGE LEFT is towards the audience or camera and to the actor's left.

The director may say to you, for example, "Move downstage right." He may say, "Move upstage center." If he uses the stage terms, you'll know what he's talking about because you're professional enough to know your business.

Some film or TV directors will use the terms "camera left" and "camera right." This terminology may confuse the beginning actor because it refers to movement to the camera's left and right respectively, not to the actor's left and right. Also, a director might use the terms "move in" or "move out." "Move in" means move more in line with the center of the lens of the camera. "Move out" means to move away from the center of the camera stance, putting you farther away from the center line of the lens.

So that you can better acquaint yourself with the stage directions, I've outlined the directions on the drawings below.

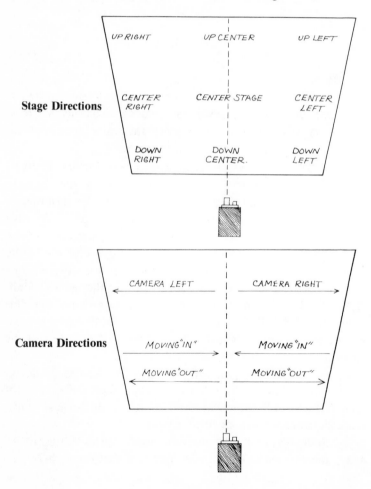

The following suggestions are only that—suggestions: they are not rules which have to be followed. When you're actually shooting or interviewing for a commercial, you should definitely follow the instructions given by the director. During the interview, however, usually you'll be pretty much on your own. The director can tell how much you've worked on camera just by your bearing—your "camera presence." You've probably heard of the term "stage presence"; the same applies to screen acting. Basically you should keep yourself in front of the camera as much as possible, and avoid turning your back to it unless directed otherwise. If the director and producer of the commercial cannot see your expressions, they won't know how effective you'll be when dealing with the viewing audience. If you don't have good camera presence, you'll make the director's job much harder on the set.

Read the following ideas and suggestions and keep them in mind. Know the rules of thumb, then you can break them when you find it necessary. But at least you'll be breaking them knowingly and not out of naivete.

Standing

In most commercial interviews, or for that matter most commercials, you will perform standing up. This is because you'll generally create more energy on your feet than you would sitting. For example, you've probably seen the energy difference between a teacher who lectures standing up and one who sits in a chair; the latter loses fire while sitting. So given a choice on an interview whether to stand or sit, I usually stand.

While standing, or in any position for that matter, watch your posture. Be careful not to slouch. Since the camera is focused in on the actor, any slouching will be greatly exaggerated; bad posture on camera looks much worse than it does in real life. Also, bad posture doesn't put you in your best "spokesman" position; you lose authority with bad posture. You're giving the audience the impression that you're weak, insincere, and less than intelligent and worldly. But, of course, there are those few times when slumping might add to the character you're portraying in the commercial. Do it because it fits the character and not because you're just too lazy to stand up straight.

It's usually best to stand with your weight evenly divided between both feet. The problem with standing with your weight on one foot and then shifting to the other foot is that in the shift, your face might go right off the screen. Also the audience will see an up and down motion while you shift from one foot to the other. Many actors don't realize how little space they have when working with the camera; a movement of just an inch could take you out of the frame. On interviews the camera is usually focused very tightly on your face, so even if you lean on one foot and don't sway from side to side, you still look unbalanced. You don't project an image of confidence in this position. An even, balanced speaking stance is usually best. But, again, weigh the situation and then make your own decisions, depending on the character you wish to portray.

If you're interviewing for the commercial with a partner, you want to avoid standing with your profile to the camera as much as possible. If you stand facing each other, with the camera pointed at both of you from the side, the audience will only see profiles. Profiles generally don't hold people's attention; the audience gets the feeling that you are hiding something. You don't seem to be on the up-and-up. It's as if the viewers were listening to someone who is looking the other way. They just don't believe that the person is being honest with them. Also, if you and your partner stand directly facing each other on the interview, the director and producer won't see your faces and won't have any idea how well you can react to the message in the commercial. They won't learn much about your acting ability. What they will learn is that you haven't worked very much with the camera and basically you don't know the ins and outs of working with a partner.

So instead of standing feet together, profile to the camera, stand very slightly turned, with your upstage foot pointing more toward your partner and your downstage foot pointing more toward the camera.

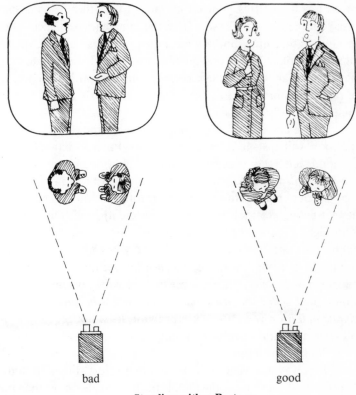

bad   good

Standing with a Partner

As you can see, this stance will open your body more towards the camera. You'll see a lot of this activity on stage and on TV shows shot in front of live audiences. It is known as "cheating" your body toward the camera (or audience). In the commercial interview you likely will have to exercise your own judgment about using this technique. In actual commercials, directors often will instruct you to "cheat."

Upstaging: You and your partner should stay on the same plane, neither of you getting closer to the camera than the other. In other words, you must be careful not to be upstaged. "Upstaging" means literally putting yourself upstage of the other person. Suppose your partner moves away from the camera (or audience), thus upstage. In that situation, you must turn your head away from the camera to look at him. Consequently, his face will be more toward the camera than yours. Remember, the camera is probably going to be right on your face, so if you turn even slightly away from it, you'll be at a disadvantage.

Some actors, and that's not to mention the one who wrote this book, will upstage actors on interviews. I'm not saying that this is a good technique, because if you get caught doing such a thing, you will look like an amateur and your partner will immediately become your enemy. However, some actors will tend to lean just a bit (not enough to look off-balance) on the upstage foot, putting them slightly upstage of their partner. If you try this, your partner will have to turn his head slightly toward you and you'll have the advantage. For one thing, the audience will see more of your face than his. For another, since his face turns to yours, the line of focus is on you. *I point this trick out so that you'll be sure not to let anyone pull it on you.* If one is a pro at it, he won't get caught. It will seem a natural shift to the upstage foot and he will be careful not to look off-balance.

If you're interviewing with two other actors, I tend to think it's better for you to be in the middle of the triangle rather than on a side, because the apex of a triangle usually gets more attention. After all, the people on both sides have to face in to you when you're talking and the lines of focus point to you. Also, if you step back just a little, you cause the other two actors to look back at you. This is not to say, however, that you won't be seen if you're on a side. You're going to have so much energy and do such a terrific job that no matter where you are, you will make yourself seen.

One very important thing to keep in mind when you're working with other actors is that you should stay very "tight."

What many actors don't realize is that the camera will separate you and your partner. The curvature of the TV lens bends around in a concave shape. Therefore, the distance between you and your partner will be exaggerated. If you ever saw your favorite TV game show being taped, you were probably amazed at how small the set actually was.

The farther apart you and your partner are, the greater the distance the camera must pull back to include both of you in the shot. The farther the camera pulls back, the smaller your faces become on the screen. Of course, while actually shooting the commercial the director will show you where to stand, but generally, as pointed out earlier, he won't give you much, if any, direction for the interview. Actually, many times actors are standing almost shoulder-to-shoulder on the interview unless for some reason this would not fit the scene they're shooting. Generally if you're almost shoulder-to-shoulder, it will appear as though you're just about the right distance from each other for regular conversation.

Sitting

If the commercial script requires that you sit at a table, remember that being behind (i.e., upstage of) it, rather than at one side, will keep you more in front of the camera.

If you're working with another actor, remember that profiles are to be avoided as much as possible. It's best for the two of you to sit at the back of the table together, which will open you both up to the camera. Sitting at the sides makes it harder to avoid profiles. Also, sitting at the sides would really put a lot of distance between the two of you, causing the camera to pull farther back.

Be careful how you sit down during the taping. Don't sit with your head leaning forward and pitched down. During that moment while you are in transition between standing and sitting, don't let the camera see the top of your head. Keep your head and shoulders upright, as will be discussed in the section on head movement.

Sitting at a Table with Another Actor

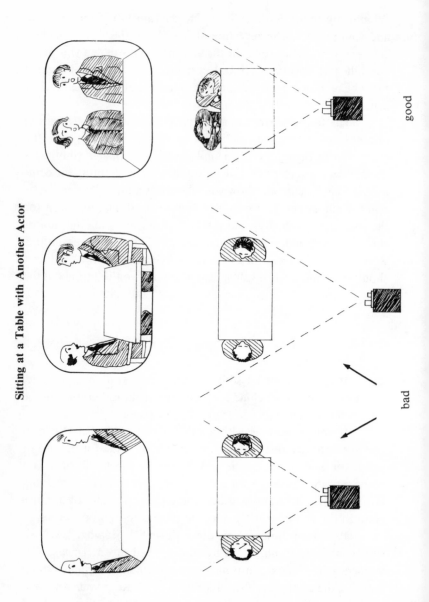

good

bad

48

When sitting, with or without a table, it's generally better to cross the upstage leg over the downstage leg, rather than the other way around. This opens your body up to the camera. If you're sitting while talking directly to the camera, it really doesn't matter how you cross your legs. This is not to say, however, that you should cross your legs at all. You'll have to use your own judgment. Whatever you do with your legs remember to be careful about your posture.

As with standing while working with another actor, remember to "cheat" toward the camera even though you're talking to your partner. The same techniques apply for talking to another actor while sitting as well as standing.

Kneeling

Rarely will you be kneeling in a commercial, but it does happen from time to time. For instance, if you're working with a child and the situation seems appropriate, it's a good idea to kneel next to him. If a child and an adult appear together in a commercial, the audience's attention is automatically drawn more to the face of the child than to that of the adult. Kneeling down to the child will help get you equal billing.

Since you want the audience to see as much of you as possible, it's better to kneel on the downstage leg, with the upstage leg bent upward. This position opens your entire body to the camera.

bad   good

Walking

Remember that the camera will exaggerate your moves, so when walking keep your steps very "small." To keep your body open to the camera, it's usually a good idea to start walking with the upstage foot as opposed to the downstage one. In other words, if you start walking from the left to the right, it's better to start on the right foot, and vice versa. (Eventually you won't even think about this, just as you really don't think about shifting your car.) But please don't get too bogged down in the technique and think that you always have to walk this way. The point is, keep in mind ways to cheat your body towards the camera.

Be careful that you don't walk with your body pitched too far forward or backward. When your body is "out of line" (as with any posture problem) it will only be exaggerated on camera.

Hitting Marks

In the theatre you can move to a "general" area on stage because being an inch off your mark usually won't make a lot of difference. This isn't the case when working with the camera. Again, the frame of the camera is very small. Let's suppose, for example, that you have to run down the street and stop in front of the camera, putting yourself exactly in the middle of the camera frame (i.e., an equal distance on both sides of your head to the edges of the frame). The lights are set for certain positions and not being in the right place can cause the lighting in the scene to be incorrect. Moreover, stopping an inch off one particular spot might throw you completely out of the frame. Often, to keep actors in the picture, directors will have marks on the floor (or sidewalk, or whatever) to show where you should stop or stand. Stopping at the correct spot is called "hitting your mark." Of course, you can't look down searching for your marks when you're moving. Eventually it will become second nature for you to "feel" your way to the marks. Please don't underestimate the importance of hitting your marks. You will ruin a shot every time you're off your mark, even if it's by only a few centimeters.

Crossing In Front of Someone

You must be careful not to turn in circles when you're crossing in front of someone. If, for example, you were on another actor's left and you crossed to his right in the normal fashion, when you got to his other side, you'd have to turn all the way around in order to be facing that person again. In order that you may avoid this, it's best to first cross in front of him, stepping very slightly upstage just after you pass, and then pivot on your upstage foot toward the camera, resuming the normal posture for talking to another actor (described earlier). This may seem a little awkward at first, but like all other odd camera moves, it will become easy with practice.

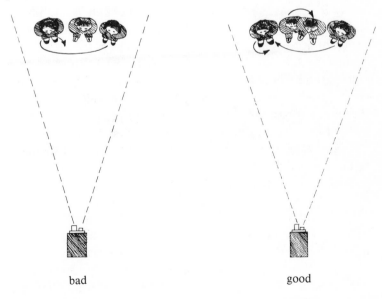

bad   good

Whenever someone is crossing in front of *you,* you should make a "counter move." This is a very small one-step move which you make in the opposite direction as the other actor passes in front of you. It's used to "counter" act your partner's move, balancing out the screen. For some reason it looks odd when someone crosses in front of another actor and that actor remains completely stationary. Let me point out that you'll make few such moves in commercial interviews because of the small-space problem, but it's a good idea to know how to handle a cross should you need to use one.

Head Movement

Getting proper head movement is one of the reasons why it's important for you to read the camera directions in the script before the interview, if they are available. Many actors tend to move their heads too much. This is especially a problem when you're speaking in an extreme close-up. If you're working with a partner, then the shot will be wider, allowing greater freedom of movement, but you still must be careful to stay in the frame. Another common problem is that of actors tilting their heads to the right or the left. If your head is tilted too much (and even a little bit can be too much!), it will angle from one bottom corner of the screen to the opposite top corner. Aside from looking silly, a tilting or bobbing head distracts the audience from your mission—to sell the product!

I'm not suggesting that you must always keep your head at a 90-degree angle to your shoulders. Certainly your head shouldn't be unnaturally stiff. The best thing to do is to practice with a video camera and watch the playback on the monitor to determine exactly how much movement you can have with certain shots.

Also, as mentioned earlier, keep your head up. You'll need to be especially conscious of this on the interview, where the lighting usually will be very poor compared with studio lighting. If you lower your head too much you will get shadows in your eyes and it will appear as though you are tired. On the other hand, don't put your head up so far that the viewer would be able to see up your nostrils.

Eyes

The eyes are extremely important in commercial advertising. You've probably heard the old saying that "the eyes are the mirror of the soul." In my opinion they are also the mirror of the commercial! Eyes are where truths and lies are revealed: You can't hide your lyin' eyes.

There must be a lot of energy in the actor's eyes. The eyes must be open and alive. Many amateur actors tend to squint their eyes when the bright lights hit them. Squinty eyes almost make it appear as though the actor has something to hide—definitely a killer in commercial advertising.

The eyes should have a gleam in them. Many beginning commercial actors let their eyelids droop. Put some tension in your eye muscles and make those eyes "jump out" to the audience.

When performing the commercial alone, you'll probably be looking right into the camera, unless otherwise directed. Be careful that you don't have what I like to call "dangling eyes" (eyes that roam around aimlessly, not looking into the camera). Eyes should have concentrated focus. This makes the actor's words more believable and sincere. You must keep in mind that the camera is the audience's eyes. How many times have you been talking to someone who was looking around the room for other people? Do you really get the feeling that that person sincerely cares about talking with you? If you're looking from right to left, and up and down while talking to the camera, in effect you're talking to someone without looking at him.

When actors forget lines, they tend to roll their eyes to the top of their heads and look up to the heavens for help. God isn't going to bring the words down to you and they aren't written on the ceiling. So if you're in an interview for a commercial and forget your lines, just keep looking forward, regain your composure, and go on. Looking up in the air just tells the people for whom you're interviewing that you're screwing up. If you just pause, keep your focus on the camera, and go on, they will, at worst, think you paused a little too long.

Many actors, especially those just starting out, have the feeling that during the taping part of the audition they should be speaking towards the people sitting in the room—*a big mistake.* Rarely will the people actually casting the commercial be in the interview. The people who will ultimately cast it will watch the videotapes at a later time. If you're looking off to one side of the camera, the people who watch the tapes later won't have the feeling that you are communicating with them (and thus with any TV audience), and you won't come off as being sincere. (Exceptions: Sometimes during the taping part of the audition, someone asks you questions; if that is the case, it is generally okay for you to look at that person as you answer. On occasion the entire taping part of the interview will consist not of your performing a commercial but of your answering some questions about yourself while the camera is rolling; when that happens, look at the person who is asking you questions unless otherwise instructed.)

Smiling

You'll probably have little chance of getting into commercials if it appears as though you took smiling lessons from Mike Wallace. In almost all commercial acting, you can't overdo smiles. Of course, you have to read over the script and decide whether your character would be smiling, but many, many, times, commercial characters are "all smiles." Smiles sell, and they sell big!

Gesturing

It's generally better to gesture with the upstage hand (the hand farthest away from the camera) rather than the downstage one if you're not standing directly facing the camera. Obviously, if you're working by yourself facing the camera it really won't matter which hand you use. But when you're facing another actor it is important to gesture with the hand that will not cover you. This isn't to say that you can't ever use the downstage hand, just that you should keep in mind the possible effect and practice the general rule.

Be careful about sticking your hand straight out in front of you and pointing at the camera. Because there's no depth of field on camera, this gesture will make you appear as though you have a short stubby hand. The camera lens does not see the distance between the finger and the body; it all appears two-dimensional. There are times, however, when it's appropriate for you to point, and you'll have to be the judge of those times when interviewing.

Keep in mind the principles above, but don't *plan* your gestures; when you do they usually come off looking planned. In everyday life we don't think about what to do with our hands. We concentrate on the meaning of what we're saying and our gestures flow naturally from our thoughts. I'm not sure why it is that many actors say, "But what do I do with my hands?" I say to them, "Don't do anything." In everyday life when you're yelling at someone, for example, do you think to yourself, "Now, what gestures can I use to show my anger?" You just do it! You're concentrating so hard on what you're trying to communicate that gestures become second nature. Also, many actors think that they *always* have to be gesturing with their hands. Nonsense. Again, we get back to *observation*. Notice that people aren't always gesturing during conversation. USE GESTURES AS YOU NORMALLY WOULD IF YOU WERE IN THAT SITUATION. I know, you might be thinking that *you* aren't in that situation—but your *character* in the commercial is. You get your interpretation of that character from your own real-life experiences and from your observations of others.

As time passes and you work more with the camera, your movements will become second nature. Just remember—though the commercial should contain a lot of energy, make that energy appear in your face and eyes instead of in big *physical* movements. You don't have to jump up and down waving your arms. Energy doesn't necessarily mean external exuberance, it can also mean the internal excitement shown in your attitude.

Working With the Set

Learn subtle ways to cheat your body towards the camera by watching the way actors in commercials work with the sets. Sometimes you'll have to work on camera in ways that seem quite unnatural in real life, but in the commercial these actions appear normal. This section doesn't cover all instances of working with particular sets in particular situations, but highlights a couple of the most common props and jobs that you'll find in commercials.

For example, when washing walls, windows, counters, etc., it's best to turn your body towards the camera or about halfway from the wall to the camera. If you wipe the surface in the manner in which you normally would, your back will face the camera. Though that action may seem the most "natural," believe me the audience won't think so from their vantage point!

When using a telephone, it's generally better to use the upstage side of your face instead of the downstage side. When you put the phone up against the downstage side of your face, you tend to cover your face. Also, it's important to keep the phone an inch or so below your mouth. This will open your mouth up to the audience and keep the conversation from becoming garbled into the phone. As usual, there are exceptions. For example, it might be that you are portraying a character who is placing a secretive telephone call. Then there would be reason to cover your mouth with the phone. But then you must be *extremely* careful not to mumble the dialogue into the phone.

I would like to add a side note which really doesn't fit into the category of physical staging, but since we're talking about using a phone, it deserves mention. When you're talking on the phone, give the imagined person on the other end of the line adequate time to "talk back." Many actors tend to rush through dialogue on the phone and fail to react to what is being said on the other end of the line! This is a true sign of an amateur actor who can't concentrate on the situation. On the other hand, you shouldn't pause long enough for the conversation to come off as too slowly paced. But do at least allow enough time to make the conversation believable. Be sure to react to what the other person supposedly is saying. It's quite rare that you'll actually hear someone on the other end of the line (either offstage or off camera). Usually none of the phones on sets or stages work, but it's up to you to make it look as though they do!

* * *

At the outset these guidelines (they are not rules) might seem somewhat mechanical. You will have to practice them many times before they become a part of your repertoire. But, in time, they will become more natural to you and you will have acquired what is very important to every actor in the screen medium—good "camera presence."

Chapter Five

The Hero

Any role you get in a commercial is a supporting role. Remember that the most important thing in any commercial is the *product,* not the actor. Advertisers want you to sell yourself only insofar as it enhances the selling of their product. The product is NUMERO UNO.

As such, it deserves its own special chapter in this book. Of course, you'll want to be sure you understand the terms and techniques in the preceding chapters. Then you can more effectively focus your attention and energies on four aspects of dealing with the product, or "hero," explained in this chapter.

Using Substitution

Let's suppose you're cast in a commercial where you must eat ice cream. You're all excited about the job and you arrive on the set in plenty of time for makeup, wardrobe, etc. You rehearse the scene. The property person brings you the ice cream cone that you are supposed to eat and enjoy during the commercial. He tells you not to eat it until you actually shoot a take so he won't have to keep getting new ice cream cones for each shot.

The script says you are supposed to eat the ice cream and show on your face how much you like it. It won't be hard for you to be very convincing; you really do love ice cream.

The cameras roll and the director yells "Action." This time you're really going to eat the ice cream. The scene goes great until the point where you actually have to eat it. You take one bite and spit it out, choking with disbelief. What happened? It sure didn't taste like ice cream to you. As a matter of fact, it tasted more like lumpy mashed potatoes with a little food coloring added. Huh?

The director informs you that on a commercial set it would be difficult to use real ice cream because the lights would melt it before you had a chance to take a bite. You're really puzzled at this point. What are you going to do? Let's suppose you personally hate lumpy mashed potatoes on a cone. You're definitely in a bind. The director wants you to shoot the ad many, many times over again and you just can't bring yourself to like the taste even once, much less for all the other takes.

But you will eat mashed potatoes and love it. Nobody said it was going to be easy, but I hope my hints on "substitution" in Chapter 1 will make it a little easier to enjoy distasteful products, or distasteful props, as in the example above.

Because of the "truth in advertising" laws, if the commercial were actually for an ice cream company or if the ice cream were an integral part of the commercial (for instance, someone says, "Our hair dryer won't melt ice cream"), then the ice cream would have to be real. Oh, so now you think in that case you won't have to worry about substituting—you *like* the real product. Think again.

I remember shooting a McDonald's commercial in which I had to take two bites of a cheeseburger. Keep in mind that they may do one hundred takes or more for a commercial, so you can imagine how many bites of cheeseburgers I had to take! Now, personally I love cheeseburgers, but after a couple hundred bites, the cheeseburgers started to taste like Gainsburgers. And I had to concentrate on being very hungry when, in fact, I had eaten enough cheeseburgers to feed the city of Cincinnati. SUBSTITUTION got me through it all.

Using the substitution technique you can "psyche" yourself into liking just about anything. It doesn't matter if you really like what you're selling. You're an actor; pretending is part of your job. (Any moral objections you may have to a particular product are between you and your conscience. You can always refuse a job offer.) Remember, no matter what anyone says, the bottom line is *what's up on the screen.* The audience doesn't care what's going on in each actor's mind as long as the performance is convincing. The McDonald's corporation doesn't care if you're concentrating on eating pudding, for example, when you're actually eating a cheeseburger in one of their commercials. Their concern is how the commercial appears to the public.

Mentioning the Product Name

One of the most important things to do when interviewing for a commercial role or performing a commercial is to MAKE THE NAME OF THE PRODUCT STAND OUT FROM THE REST OF THE SCRIPT. THIS IS THE WHOLE POINT OF THE COMMERCIAL! The audience should walk away from that commercial at least remembering the name of the product. There are several ways to accomplish this. One is to say the name of the product just a little louder than you do the rest of the commercial script. Be careful, however, not to overdo this; you don't want to be obvious about it.

Another way to make the product name stand out is to treat it differently in tone or pace from the rest of the words. You might be talking in a high tone of voice and then drop your voice slightly when you mention the product name, returning to the high voice when reading the rest of the commercial, or if you're talking fairly rapidly while saying the dialogue, you slow down slightly when you get to the product name.

Pausing is a very effective tool, also. When a speaker wants to emphasize a certain point, he can pause right before he makes the point. This gives the audience time to gather the information already presented and to get ready for the next set of ideas. Say a sentence aloud, and pause before the most important word in the sentence. You'll notice how that word stands out. Pausing right after the product name can sometimes have the same effect. MAKE THE AUDIENCE REMEMBER THE PRODUCT NAME.

When you mention the product name, it's important that you look into the camera or at the actor you're supposed to be talking to (depending upon the setting of the commercial). You don't want to "bury" the product name while looking at the script or looking away at a Q-card. Actually, it's better to say any *line* which mentions the product name directly to the camera or to your partner. This may be difficult in an interview, when you are not very familiar with the script. With a lot of practice, you'll get better at it.

Putting the Product in Its Best Light

You should look for the words in the script which put the product in its best light and perhaps emphasize those words. For instance, take the hypothetical commercial line, "Sparkle Toothpaste helps prevent cavities." The important words here are the product name and "prevents cavities." The word "helps" is there because advertisers must be certain that every statement made in a commercial is strictly true. Say "helps" clearly, but you probably wouldn't want to give it the same prominence that you give to "prevents cavities."

Suppose we say that our product is "virtually trouble free." For you the actor, "virtually" has less importance. By emphasizing the importand words—"trouble free," you make the product name stand out in its best light.

I could go on and on with examples, but I think you get the message: look over the script very carefully, search for words that put the product in its best light, and make the product name stand out with those important words.

Handling the Product

The commercial actor must be extremely careful not to conceal the label of the product in any way. When you hold the product, make sure not even one finger covers part of the front of the package. You can hold the product from the back with your fingers on the sides, or you can hold the top of the product with one hand and the bottom part with the other. However you hold it, make sure that the product label directly faces the camera. Even holding the product just a little off to one side will usually cover part of the product name—a NO-NO!

Whether you are working alone or with another actor, it is usually best to hold the product close to, or level with, your face. Notice that in most commercials the actor will hold the product in this general area. (Of course there are thousands of exceptions. For example, in a Ford automobile commercial, you'll find very few actors holding the auto next to their faces!) With small products you don't want to hold the product too far below your face or way off to one side of it. The camera lens will naturally separate the product from you. And if you hold the product off to one side of your face, the cameraman will have to pull the camera back to get both you and the product in the shot. Therefore, your face would show up smaller. Your goal here is for the casting personnel or the TV audience to see the association between the product and you.

The viewing audience will sense how you feel about a product just by the way you hold it. Hold the product as though you really like it. You've seen people hold things as though they couldn't care less about the object. Think nice things to yourself about the product and this will help you hold it with pride.

Part Two

The *Business* of Acting in Commercials

I am frequently asked, "Which is the most important trait in attaining a successful commercial acting career—experience, talent, or luck?" My answer is usually something to the effect of, "Which is the most important leg of a three-legged stool?" We've been discussing the talent and experience aspects of the commercial acting profession. Now it's time to learn the BUSINESS aspects so that when that *lucky* break does come your way, you'll know how to handle it in a professional way.

Never forget one thing: ACTING IS A BUSINESS! Too many actors love to keep their noses in the air and think that all you need for a successful acting career is acting ability. These poor misguided souls believe that if they're talented enough, then they'll be discovered. This belief couldn't be further from the truth!

After HOW TO ACT & EAT AT THE SAME TIME was

published, I found myself speaking at numerous acting schools and universities. I was amazed at how naive many of the students were when it came to the business side of acting. One afternoon, for example, I was speaking in front of about two hundred students at a very prestigious acting school in Los Angeles. I had been speaking for about four hours on the "business" of acting when a star-struck young lady stood up in the middle of one of my sentences and yelled out, "Mr. Logan, you are a capitalist pig!"

I retorted to this girl, "I resent being called a pig." Yes, I guess I am a capitalist because I make my living from acting. But I have never thought of myself as a pig!

She went on to say, "You should act because you love your art and want to perform in front of the public for art's sake—not for the money."

"Honey, what do you do for a living?" I asked.

"I work at Denny's as a waitress."

"Do you get paid for this job?"

"Well, of course, I mean I have to pay my bills."

That's just what I wanted her to say. I looked at her with a smile and said, "But you should work at Denny's because you want to serve the public—not for the money."

"That's different," was her reply. *It's always different.* For some reason artists are considered less artistic if they get paid, as if they are compromising themselves. Where this nonsense began really escapes me. The fact that someone happens to be a good business person makes him no less talented as an artist, and in my opinion, it makes him more so!

Moreover, if you are serious about acting professionally, you cannot expect that because *you* have such terrific talent, a job offer will come out of the blue—without your having to bother with going through channels. Part Two of this book takes you through the business process: training, photos, resumes, agents, unions, interviews, and commercial business practices. If you know what to expect both during the job interview and on the job, you can prevent a lot of mistakes and heartaches.

Chapter Six

Getting Started

Training

Many actors have the impression that commercial acting just comes naturally. Wrong. Maybe acting comes naturally to you, but as you have probably learned from this book, "natural" in real life doesn't always come naturally on camera.

College degrees, in and of themselves, don't mean very much to commercial producers. Many motion picture film school graduates, for example, who are working at such places as Photo-Mat Drive-ins will testify to that fact. However, a college degree could be valuable to you if you obtained good acting experience on the college stage. And if you learned confidence from these productions, then the experience was well worth it.

You can get acting experience anywhere. Almost every town has school and community theatre productions. If yours doesn't, then you can start your own theatre group to get acting experience. The point is, one doesn't have to be in Los Angeles, Chicago, or New York to gain experience. If you ever do plan to move to one of those cities, then the local experience will prove invaluable to you.

A commercial acting workshop is really a must for any actor who hasn't worked in the commercial field before, especially in the major markets where there's more competition. Acting in commercials is different from acting in other forms of the media. For example, learning how to handle products, how to give out boring information while making it sound interesting, how to work in a small time frame, etc., are areas which are usually unfamiliar to the inexperienced commercial actor. Even the experienced actor will find commercials a different ball game altogether, though he will have excellent groundwork for working in commercials.

A commercial workshop doesn't have to be in one of the major markets either. You can start with one in your local area. Numerous modeling schools all across the country offer commercial acting classes. Later, if you do decide to move to a major commercial market, you can take another commercial class in *that* area to better acquaint yourself with the personnel in the business there, etc.

If you're looking for a commercial class in an area outside of the Major Cities (defined in SAG and AFTRA commercial contracts as Los Angeles, Chicago, and New York), you can start looking for a school by checking with other actors in your area. Personal references are always best. If there are any commercial agents in your area, then check with them also. Photographers might be able to give you some recommendations as well; since they work with actors and models, they can guide you to the school which seems to be turning out the best students. Call your local TV and radio station(s) to find out what school(s) they contact when they're looking for commercial actors. As a last resort you can check the yellow pages of the telephone directory. Check around to find out about each school's reputation. You can start with the Better Business Bureau.

In quite a few of the smaller cities there may be no commercial workshops. In these cases, there apparently isn't as much call for one as in other cities. However, this is not to say that you can't check the surrounding areas for such a workshop. If you are unable to find a commercial workshop in your area, or surrounding areas, study the beginning of this book over and over again and practice on your own, though this book should really be used as an aid to a commercial workshop rather than just a substitute.

In Los Angeles you can find out about commercial workshops by looking through issues of *Drama-Logue* and *Entertainment Monthly,* and if you're in New York you can use *Back Stage* and *Show Business.* Now, a word of caution. Some of the workshops listed in these publications are good and many of them are not. Check with commercial agents and your actor friends to see whom they recommend.

Whether you're seeking commercial classes in your local area or one of the major markets, you should be able to decide on a few good workshops which seem right for you. But I wouldn't just "sign up." *Before you enroll,* audit some classes. You wouldn't buy a car without test-driving it around the block first, and you shouldn't enroll in a commercial acting class without observing a session first. If a particular school won't let you audit a class, I'd start looking for another school. Also, if the commercial acting class doesn't use video equipment, look for one that does. Video recording is the only effective way to analyze your performance. Black-and-white playback is sufficient.

Also, check out the teacher's qualifications. Has he actually been in commercials himself? It's hard for someone to teach people how to drive a car if he hasn't actually driven one himself. The same goes for commercial acting, so you'll probably want your teacher to have commercial acting experience. There are exceptions, of course. Many casting directors, directors, and others in the field are extremely capable of teaching commercial acting because of their positions. Just make sure the teacher is qualified.

KEEP IN MIND THAT YOU SHOULD BE EXTREMELY LEERY OF ANY SCHOOL THAT PROMISES YOU WORK. NO ONE CAN GUARANTEE YOU COMMERCIAL WORK. So scrutinize carefully any school that makes you that promise.

Photos

When you've developed the self-confidence and obtained the training and experience necessary for a successful acting career, you are ready to move on to another essential: great photos of yourself. Local TV-station ad men, casting directors, directors, and commercial producers see many, many photos every day. Make sure yours jump out and grab their attention.

If you're working in an area outside of the major markets, it's always best to check around with people in your town—TV ad men, advertising agency people, photographers, modeling school personnel, etc.—to see what the norm is concerning the types of photos you need. Whether you're working locally or in the major markets, high school yearbook photos and play production stills simply won't do. You need to go to a professional photographer who shoots actors for a living; seek recommendations from other actors and agents. In the smaller markets it might be hard to obtain such a specialized photographer, so you may want to check around to see which commmercial photographers do most of the actors' photos in that town.

If you're moving to one of the major markets, don't use the photos taken by your local photographer; those shots should be used in your local area only. Wait until you get to the city in which you plan to act to get your new photos. Photographers generally don't know what is currently selling in other markets. Many New York actors who move to Los Angeles, for example, find out that their photos are not suited for the new market.

Once you've received the names of a few good photographers, go to their studios and see some of their work, preferably photos of actors. Don't just take their word for it that they do good work. If they show you "artsy" photos of actors, I'd check around for other photographers. *You* want to stand out, not the photo itself. And be careful about the price. You don't want to be cheap when it comes to getting good photos, but if you have to cash a bond to pay the photographer's fee, you're probably paying too much.

The photographer might try to talk you into shooting a whole composite, which is *eventually* what you *might* need. A composite is a group of photos, usually one on the front and four or five on the back of an 8½-by-11 inch sheet of graphic paper. Commercial agents show composites to casting directors in order to get interviews for their client actors.

My personal opinion is that when you're just starting out and are without an agent, you don't need a composite. If you set up a composite and the agent you eventually end up with doesn't like one of the photos, you'll have to make another whole composite. Also, some commercial agents don't use composites, though most of them do. My best advice is to get a good "head shot" for starters. Even if you are in an area where most commercial work is non-union and agents are not used, you probably should not start out with a composite; sending a head shot to local TV ad people is usually fine unless your specific area generally uses composites. Since it differs from area to area in the smaller markets, check with the TV ad people and other actors. In any case, get your head shot first; later, after you've developed a better feel for the market, you can consider getting a composite.

A "head shot" is just that—a photo of your face, usually from about the shoulders up. You should be looking directly into the camera for such a shot. Photos which have half your face in the dark or profiled simply won't do. Commercial producers, directors, and casting directors want to see all of your face in the head shot.

It's important that there be nothing distracting in the background of your head shot. The commercial head shot should be taken outdoors, or in a natural setting if it's indoors, i.e., grocery store, bank, etc. (no phony indoor backdrops, please). Parks make terrific settings because the background is usually distant enough to be out of focus so that it doesn't distract from your face. Don't have anything in the photo that barks, moos, quacks, chirps, or looks hungry. Animals will definitely take the focus off of you.

The essential thing here is for your face to be the center of attention. For that reason, do not wear distracting clothes in your photograph. Nothing should be covering your face—hats, hands, jewelry, or hair. If you have good teeth, be sure to show them!

And, most importantly, you should definitely have a nice smile in your photo.

After shooting your head shot, the photographer should give you "contact sheets," known in industry jargon as "proof sheets." Use a magnifying glass or "lupe" to view the small proofs. This will enable you to get an idea what they'll look like when blown up. Be sure to have other people look at the proofs also. Between you and your photographer, actor friends, acting coach, etc., you should be able to find a few proof shots which everyone seems to like. (Note: If you already have an agent, then your agent should definitely be the one to pick your photos. After all, it's his job to "sell" your talents.)

Be sure that the photos you decide to blow up look like you. If they don't, then you're cutting your own throat two ways:

1. When you actually get into the interviewer's office (TV or ad agency person, agent, casting director, director, or producer) you won't look like the person in the photo you sent. You will have misrepresented yourself. The interviewer wanted someone who looked like the person in the photo you sent or he wouldn't have called you into his office in the first place. Since you don't really fit the type he was looking for, you have wasted his time and yours. Conversely, the interviewer might not call you in after looking at your photo because the photo shows a type that he isn't presently interested in interviewing. Perhaps he would have been interested in you as you actually look, but you lost out because you didn't accurately represent yourself.

2. The person interviewing you might be seeing many people in a few hours, and the photo reminds him who you are. The interviewer may remember what you look like, but if you don't resemble the person in your photo, he can't match your face to a name—your photo has defeated your purpose.

After you have made a few eight-by-tens from the better proofs, have other people look them over to choose a single favorite. As with the proof sheets, you don't want to be the only one in the decisionmaking process.

Example of a Head Shot, A

TERESA BROWN

Photo by Buddy Rosenberg

Example of a Head Shot, B

BLAKE HIGGINS

Photo by Buddy Rosenberg

Example of a Head Shot, C

LILLIAN ADAMS

Photo by Olivier de Courson

Example of a Head Shot, D

Morgan Webb

Photo by Kirby Sires

Example of a Composite, Side One

PHIL MANN

Photo by Tama Rothschild

Example of a Composite, Side Two

PHIL MANN

Photos by Tama Rothschild

Once you have selected a head shot, take it to a duplicating store which is designed especially for duplicating photos. If you are in New York, Los Angeles, or Chicago, you can find plenty of these types of outlets designed especially for actors. Check around with others to find out which ones do the best work. In the smaller markets you can find out about duplicating stores from the usual people who deal with actors. You can also check the yellow pages under "Photo Finishing." But before you commission a company to duplicate your photos, look at other photos they have mass-produced. After all, it does you absolutely no good to spend big bucks getting a head shot if the duplication is poor.

In the Major Cities you'll need at least a hundred of these head shots to start out, fewer in the smaller markets. And note that most agents prefer to have the head shot on gloss or pearl paper. Some of the duplicating stores put your name on the photo, which is *extremely important.* I think it's best to have it printed on a whited-out space at the bottom of the photo in black lettering. That way, the name really stands out. Some people have their name printed directly on the bottom part of the image, but I think the name tends to get lost in the picture if it's printed in this manner. Also, don't use fancy script writing for your name; it's too hard to read. Block lettering is best.

—When You Are Ready for a Composite

You may want to have a composite made up after you find an agent; a composite gives the casting personnel a better idea of how you "look" and photograph than does a single photo. You should have different expressions, poses, clothes, etc., in the shots to show versatility (see the sample head shots and composite here). I'd be careful, however, about showing totally different "types" in your composite. It's okay to vary your image somewhat, but if you show four or five distinctly different types in the same composite, then you're going to confuse the casting personnel. After looking at a composite many casting directors want to walk away with a feeling of what type of characters you can play. If the composite contains many conflicting "looks" and types, then he doesn't know how to place you. Of course, in the future there's nothing to stop you from having more than one compsite, which would enable you to show distinctly different types on different composites. But let's just face it, when it comes to commercials, you're primarily going to play the type of characters which fit your physical looks.

If you have any special skills, such as riding a unicycle, then you can display that in your composite if you make one. Also, if you have great hands, you might want to show those in a composite. This is especially true in the smaller markets where there aren't as many specialized models who just do hand modeling.

The Resume

Commercial agents rarely use an actor's resume to help get him into commercial interviews, especially in the major markets. However, most commercial agents want to see what you've done in the acting profession before taking you on as a client. In the smaller markets, TV ad men want to see what acting experience you've had.

The resume shouldn't contain information which isn't related directly to acting. Commercial agents, for instance, don't care about your past employment if that employment wasn't in the acting profession. And, similarly, they don't care about your schooling, except in the area of acting.

Use list form; don't write out sentences. Agents and casting personnel should be able to glance at your resume and learn the important facts immediately. And for the same reason, list your most important credits first. Forget chronological order—you don't even need to show dates. Most people who will be looking at your resume will be in a hurry and might not get past the first credit or two. The person who writes his resume in sentence structure usu-

Sample Resume

```
                         Joe South          (Home address is optional
                    5555 West Street         when seeking representa-
                  Hollywood, CA 00000        tion.  Once you have an
                     (213)555-9999           agent, however, never
                  Srv. (213)555-0000         list your address--list
                                             your agent's.)


 Height:  5'8"                               Eyes:  Blue
 Weight:  150                                Hair:  Blonde
                                             SAG - AFTRA


TELEVISION

  THREE'S COMPANY            (Co-star)    ABC
  DALLAS                     (Feature)    CBS

FILM

  BEACH GIRLS                (Co-star)    Crown Int'l Pictures

COMMERCIALS

  LIST AVAILABLE UPON REQUEST

STAGE ROLES

  ROOMIES                    Bert         Atlanta Community Theatre
  WAITING FOR GODOT          Estragon     University of Arkansas

THEATRICAL TRAINING

  Bill Jacobs Acting Workshop             Atlanta, Georgia
  University of Arkansas                  Fayetteville, Arkansas
  Jim Daniels Performing Workshop         Hollywood, California

SPECIAL ABILITIES

  Snow skiing
  Surfing
  Guitar
  Scuba diving


            (Note:  If you do not have any credits under a
            certain category, do not list that category.)
```

ally does so to make it look longer than it warrants. But actors shouldn't forget that the purpose of the resume is to communicate, and writing out long sentences to "pad" the resume only obstructs that communication.

The biggest obstruction to communication on the resume is outright lying. DON'T LIE ON YOUR RESUME. Eventually someone reading your resume is likely to check your credits and you'll probably never get a job with that person if you have lied. Not only that, but during some interview you'll be so busy trying to cover up the lies that you won't give a good, honest interview. The people who are casting the commercial might be looking for "new faces" anyway. If you list on your resume that you've been in many, many commercials your future employers might think you're overexposed in the commercial field. (Nothing will kill the success of a commercial faster than the audience's seeing actors they've seen before in dozens of other commercials—reminding the audience that they are actors. This is especially true for local commercials in the smaller markets.) So, it's best not even to list the commercials in which you *have* performed, much less lie. Under the heading of Commercials, most actors just write "LIST AVAILABLE UPON REQUEST." (See the sample resume here.)

Things Your Resume Should *Not* Contain

1. Your age or "age range." (Exception: If you're under eighteen years of age, then your birthdate should be on the resume to let them know that you're a minor.)

2. School acting awards. (Exception: You're in a very small market and the award will give you credibility.)

3. Personal references (acting or otherwise).

4. Occupations other than acting.

5. Personal ambitions.

6. Your personal ideas about the acting profession.

7. Astrological signs. (If your moon is in Cincinnati, fine, but leave the resume for more pertinent information.)

8. Schooling other than college, acting schools, or professional acting workshops.

9. "Extra" credits. Agents and casting personnel don't care if you were a spear shaker. (Exception: In many of the smaller markets listing extra credits might be to your advantage. It's best to check with the people in your area.)

10. Commercial acting credits (for reasons discussed above).

Things Your Resume *Should* Contain

1. Name, address (optional), and telephone number (including answering service number). Once you have an agent, delete your home address and phone number; list your agent's name (or agency), office address, and phone number.

2. Height, weight, hair color, eye color.

3. Acting unions of which you're a member. (Exception: You have so many professional credits that it's obvious you're a member of the appropriate unions.)

4. Acting credits.

5. Acting schools and workshops you've attended.

6. Special abilities. These can come in very handy. Many times producers need someone who can perform a certain skill. An actor might be cast in a commercial simply because he can perform a particular skill required for that specific commercial. Singing and dancing are very important skills, but don't list them unless you do them well. If, for example, you took singing lessons but quit them because of your throat (the teacher threatened to cut it), then I'd be

careful about listing singing as a skill. Other examples of special abilities are: water and snow skiing, surfing, motorcycle driving, and horseback riding.

Note: If you have any special medical problems such as arthritis or asthma, you should inform your agent (verbally—don't list illnesses on your resume), because some commercials require the use of someone who actually has a certain condition—"truth in advertising" laws. Don't carry this too far, however; you don't want to let the agent in on all of your illnesses to the point that he thinks you are too sick to work! And telling him you have herpes, for example, is giving him a little too much information. Just observe commercials to see what types of medications are advertised.

If you have very little to list on your resume, it's controversial whether you should even send one to a commercial agent in the first place, though I think it's usually a good idea. Some people would say not to send one, in hopes that the agent will be very interested in your type (which he sees in your photograph) and call you in, even though you might not have a lot of credits. That's a decision you'll have to make. But if you don't have any credits, then get some. You can't expect producers to hire inexperienced actors. If you walked into American Airlines and applied to be a pilot and had never flown a plane, you wouldn't get hired. The same is basically true for acting, though there are of course exceptions (such as for special abilities that a particular commercial may call for—see No. 6 of "Things Your Resume *Should* Contain," above).

You'll need as many copies of your resume as you have photos. You don't have to take out a bank loan to pay for the resume printing. Nice, clean photocopies at one of those "quickie" photocopy stores are fine, but don't get cheapy-looking reproductions. I advise against having the resumes expensively typeset; it appears as though you aren't working very much. Actors who work regularly have to change their resume frequently and typesetting

Sample Cover Letter

```
                    Susan Smith
                 2222 North Street
                 Anywhere, CA 00000


                                    [date]


Mr. Johnny Shark
The Shark Agency
4444 Any Street
Hollywood, CA 00000

Dear Mr. Shark:

    I am interested in commercial representation
with your agency.

    Thank you very much for taking the time to look
over my enclosed photo and resume.  I hope to hear
from you soon.

                            Sincerely,


                            Susan Smith


Enclosures:  Photo and resume
```

looks too permanent. I also advise against having your resume printed directly on the back of your photo, for the same reason. (Some people have their credits printed directly on their composite but, again, it just appears as though your acting jobs are very infrequent.) I've found that actors who work constantly simply type their resume neatly on white paper and have it photocopied. Staple the resumes to the backs of your photos so that when you turn the photos over, the resumes show; in other words, back to back.

Next, you need a cover letter to accompany your head shot and resume. A cover letter should be short and to the point. Simply inform the agent that you are seeking representation. (See the sample cover letter here.) Paper-clip your letter onto your stapled photo and resume. Now you have a nice little package all about you, ready to send to union-franchised agents. (See Chapter 9 for information about the appropriate people to whom you send your package in nonunion situations.)

Chapter Seven

Obtaining An Agent

In some of the smaller markets, commercials may be non-union and there may not be any union-franchised agents for actors. In that case, you might be acting as your own agent and some of the information below may not apply to you specifically. But keep in mind that most of the same rules apply for whomever you deal with to get a commercial acting job. Each area has its own peculiarities, but you can use the information here as a general guideline. (Also see Chapter 10 for more discussion on being your own agent in the smaller markets.)

In the Major Cities, trying to get commercial work without the aid of an agent is like selling Blue Cross to Humpty Dumpty—it's a waste of time. Although "freelancing" is a little more common in the markets outside of Los Angeles, you still should have an agent to get you into commercial interviews. There are so many commercials being cast that it's virtually impossible for an actor to find out about most of them. And even if you could keep track of all the interviews, you would not be able to get yourself into very many them, if any.

You can obtain lists of union-franchised agents from SAG and AFTRA offices either in person or by sending them a self-addressed stamped envelope and a dollar or so. The amount may change and may vary from office to office, so it's best to check with the office you plan to write or visit. See Appendix B for lists of union offices and their addresses.

Before attempting to contact any agents, you must obtain an answering service. There are many different kinds available. Some actors use answering machines, which are usually more reliable than are third-party answering services. But there are advantages and disadvantages to any type. Just be sure you get *some* sort of answering service, because you can't afford to miss a single call!

Getting an agent to represent you is tough. A legit agent (one who is franchised by the appropriate union) only makes ten percent of what you make. (Any agent who asks for money up front isn't legit.) Therefore, the agent has to believe you'll make money, or you'll be wasting his time.

The Big Search

The easiest way to obtain an agent is to get a friend who has an agent to set up an interview for you with that person. If you use another actor as a contact, be sure to check with him first and make sure that he and his agent are on good terms. NEVER USE SOME-ONE ELSE'S NAME UNLESS YOU HAVE CHECKED WITH HIM FIRST! In the smaller markets where there are fewer agents, personal contacts are easier to use than in the major markets where agents handle so many actors and don't know most of them on a personal basis. If an agent takes you on by another actor's reco-mendation, make sure he is representing you because he really wants to, not as a favor to your friend! An agent has to really like *you* before he can be effective.

The above method of getting into an agent's office is the ideal, but definitely not the norm. Usually actors have to go through a more grueling procedure. Whatever you do, don't just phone the agents on the list. First, send them your photo, resume, and cover letter. *Do not fold your package;* simply use an envelope large enough to house your material. Usually a 9-by-12 inch one is sufficient. If you don't hear from the agents within a week after sending your packages, you can phone them; odds are that you won't hear from any of them. When you phone, explain that you sent them a photo and resume and would like to know if you could set up a "general interview." Most of them will say "NO!" As a matter of fact, they may all say "NO!" In a month or so you can send them another package. Why keep sending them packages? Well, as the months go by, their situations may change, especially in the larger markets. For example, perhaps when you sent your package the first time, a particular agent already had plenty of actors who were your type. But a few months later those actors may have left that agent, in which case he may be more responsive to you.

Agents might decide not to represent you for any number of other reasons: For example, you may not have enough credits, or you may not be a member of the acting unions (covered in detail in the next chapter). The list of reasons not to represent you goes on and on. Whatever the problem is in your case, *don't take it personally*.

In case the photo and resume routine doesn't work for you right away, you should be prepared to use some of the other options available—such as getting film on yourself and performing in local plays or showcases.

It's always a good idea to get some "film on yourself," that is, a short scene on videotape showing your acting ability. The scene should be no longer than three to five minutes and should be recorded on, or transferred to, ¾" *videotape*, though it's still often referred to as having "film on yourself."

The tape will possibly be very helpful to you when obtaining an agent. You should make a few duplicates. Never give an original to anyone; chances are the person you're giving it to will be looking at many other tapes and yours might get lost in the shuffle.

One advantage of having tape of yourself is that it will show how you look on camera as well as your acting ability. Another advantage is that you can drop your tape off at an agent's office *in person*, though there's no guarantee that the agent will view it or even that the secretary will accept it. But chances are that the agent might view it when he has a few minutes at a future date and you can check with him periodically by phone to see if he has done so. After he has viewed it or refused to view it, you can pick it up in person. Of course the tape is no substitute for the photo and resume, which should accompany it.

In many local markets an excellent way to get some tape of yourself is to do some volunteer acting in television Public Service Announcements (PSAs). Check with your local libraries, charities, museums, etc., or simply watch some TV to see what local groups are mentioned in the PSAs (you'll probably find most of these airing late at night, but occasionally in other time periods). Many of these organizations are on the lookout for actors to help them out, and some of them actively seek actors from local theatre productions/groups. By performing in these PSAs you'll get not only some tape of yourself, but also *experience* to help you when you go for the all-important interview for your first *paying* commercial.

If your community is served by a cable TV system, you also might find some opportunities for getting tape of yourself there. Check with the cable company's Programming Director and Advertising Director, and with the local Public Access Coordinator.

If you haven't had any professional roles from which you can obtain film/tape, then try to get into a university production. In New York or Los Angeles, you can obtain information about these university film/tape productions from the trade papers discussed earlier. In the smaller cities, simply call the local college film or drama departments to find out when they will be having auditions. However, if you get film/tape from a less-than-professional source, make sure it's *good* film on yourself. Also, make sure you have dialogue. Seeing you standing around in a crowd won't convince anyone of your acting talents.

Another option is that of having a prospective agent see you act in person. Many agents attend plays around town. So, get cast in a play and send invitations to commercial agents inviting them to see you perform. Also, in the larger markets, check around town to see what theatre groups may be having "showcases" for agents, casting directors, producers, etc. Many showcases consist only of scenes, not full plays. You will perform with another actor for about three to five minutes. Those few minutes are much easier to perfect than is an entire play. Additionally, some agents slip into a coma when watching long plays for hours at a time since they usually know within a few minutes if you're right for their agency.

Lastly, just because you've sent your photos and resumes to agents and haven't heard back from them doesn't mean that you should stop trying to contact them, as pointed out earlier. Keep working on those agents even though you're trying other avenues for reaching them.

The Agent Interview

One day you'll be sitting at home and you'll receive an unexpected phone call from an agent (local TV ad person, etc.) who, after viewing your package, wants to see you for an interview. He may or may not ask you to bring in memorized material to perform. If an agent wants you to bring in prepared material, he will most likely notify you in advance. However, just to be safe, I'd have a very short (two to three minutes) monologue to perform. The monologue should not be heavy Shakespearean material. It should be light and humorous.

Most agents who want you to bring in material to perform will want you to have a two-person scene prepared; you will provide the other person. Here's a word of advice concerning the choice of the two-person scene: Be sure to pick the scene before you choose your partner. Pick a scene that fits *you,* then find the person who will play the other part. If you choose your partner first, you then have to find a scene to fit both of you; that's an added obstacle because the scene that is perfect for you might not be perfect for the partner you have chosen in advance.

Whereas in the smaller markets prepared material may be the norm, in the major markets "cold readings" are more often used. Cold readings are readings for which there is little, if any, preparation time. These impromptu readings are used in agent interviews because casting directors do not send the audition material in advance to actors who are interviewing for a particular commercial. Since cold readings are used for casting, it stands to reason that agents are more interested in your cold reading abilities than in your polished performances, though both are important.

When meeting with an agent, be sure to bring your tape (if available) and plenty of copies of your head shot and resume. Also, it's a good idea to bring all of the proof sheets from which you chose your eight-by-ten head shot. The agent might not like the head shot that you have chosen, and he might want to make another selection should he decide to represent you. Also, they will give him a better idea of how you photograph.

Dress neatly and cleanly; agents realize that what is felt on the inside shows on the outside. If you look as though you talked back to a witch doctor, the agent thinks you are a loser, someone he wouldn't want to represent. If you lose five pounds when you take off your makeup, then you're wearing too much. You don't appear very natural with gobs of makeup on your face. And guys, beards and mustaches don't sell well in the advertising world. Clean shaven people work much more in commercials than do hairy types. Your hair should also be neat; it shouldn't appear as though you dressed in front of an airplane propeller, although I realize that in Hollywood, at least, looking ridiculous is in fashion.

The clothes you wear to the commercial interview should be casual but reserved. Shirts or blouses that are so loud they could jam enemy radar are a no-no because they take the central focus off of you. You want to appear as natural as possible. After all, with most commercial work the public has to see you as "the person off the street." If you don't look like an average person, the audience might lose identity with the commercial. So, if you're female and your breasts can be seen from the space shuttle, don't accentuate that. If the only thing holding up your dress is a city ordinance, then attention will probably be attracted to the wrong area. And the guys shouldn't wear shirts unbuttoned to the navel and pants that look as if they've been spray-painted on.

If you are fortunate enough to get a description of the commercial (or the "type" to be used in it), of course you can reflect that in the way you dress for the interview. For instance, if the commercial is for a glamorous product and you happen to be the glamorous type, or if you're auditioning for a commercial to be shot on the beach and you have a nice body, take this into consideration.

BE ON TIME! This seems simple enough, but you'd be surprised how many actors turn up a few minutes late for interviews. What are you showing an agent if you turn up late for an interview? You're showing him that you aren't a very responsible individual and that you're not serious about the acting profession. There are no excuses for being late, except, of course, death—*yours*. In the case of a real tragedy, excluding your death, you should at least have the common courtesy to call the agent and inform him of the problem. "Heavy traffic" is no excuse. Keep in mind that traffic in Los Angeles and New York, for example, is very slow—you could get a parking ticket just driving crosstown. Leave your home in plenty of time for the interview.

Relax on the interview. The agent probably won't be very interested in you if you're visibly nervous. He will chitchat with you to get an idea of your personality. Since so many commercials rely very heavily on the actor's individuality, BE INTERESTING. The idea here is to give the agent more than one- or two-word answers when he asks you a question. He probably isn't *that* interested in the actual answers to his questions. He wants to learn about your personality, so give answers that are long enough for him to get an idea of your uniqueness. Look around his office to see what kinds of things he's "into." A person's office generally reflects his personality, and if you know what he's like, you'll do a better job of communicating. But don't overdo your answers. Relax and speak freely, but don't chatter, especially if you're the type whose mouth goes into overdrive when you're a little nervous. You don't want to bore your interviewer.

Be careful about coming across as too eager on an interview with anyone in this business. DON'T SEEM DESPERATE. You "want" the agent or job, or you wouldn't be there. But you don't desperately "need" that agent or that job. Agents and other people in power in the acting industry don't like "hungry" actors. Think of the interview as just a meeting to see if you both would be good for each other as a working partnership. It's mutually advantageous to investigate whether you would be good for the agent *and* whether the agent would be good for you. Looking at the interview in this respect will take off some of the pressure.

After the chitchat session, the agent may have you perform a cold reading, as we discussed earlier. If he is in a great hurry, he may ask you to perform the material immediately without any preparation, but in most cases he will probably give you a few minutes to look it over before having you perform it. Also, chances are that you won't be expected to memorize it on the spot, but rather to perform with the script in your hand, since most commercials are cast in this manner.

Don't be alarmed if an agent doesn't "jump for joy" after your reading. He sees good and bad readings all day long, and odds are your reading will be somewhere in-between.

At the end of the interview, the agent may or may not know if he wants to represent you. He may want to talk it over with other agents in his office, or he might just want time to think it over himself. If it turns out that the agent wants to represent you, he may or may not want you to sign contracts (discussed in the next chapter), but he will definitely want you to leave him photos of yourself. My suggestion is not to give him too many at this point. Let's say you give him 25 photos and in six months he still has plenty left; this is the tip-off that the agent probably isn't working for you. If you give him 150 photos, on the other hand, and then in six months he has plenty left, there is really no indication whether he is sending them out. Also, if you don't give the agent a big stack of pictures, you'll probably have to return in a few months to give him more;

this gives him a chance to see your face again and puts you on his mind!

If it turns out in a few days after your interview with the agent that he *doesn't* want to represent you, fine, you'll find another agent.

Don't be surprised or upset if a particular agent isn't polite to you on the interview. As any working actor can tell you, some agents are just plain nasty. But the majority conduct themselves in a civil and professional manner. Whatever the case, be polite, nice, and courteous.

Of course you'll want to write thank-you notes to whomever you meet on interviews. It never hurts to remind them who you are. A short note will do. Some actors, especially in the larger markets, like to have photo postcards of themselves made up. This type of note reminds the person you met not only of your name, but also of your face! A final word of caution: BE NICE TO EVERYONE IN THE AGENT'S OFFICE; THE SECRETARIES OF TODAY MIGHT BE THE AGENTS OF TOMORROW.

Chapter Eight

Unions and Agency Contracts

For actors who are in the smaller markets where there are no agents or acting unions, much of the material in this chapter won't apply directly since it deals with the business of unions and actor-agency contracts. Those actors should read it anyway, in case (a) you move to an area under union jurisdiction, or (b) someone from the "big time" sees you in your local commercial, likes you, and invites you to an interview.

Unions

A Screen Actors Guild (SAG) publication states that, "The idea has been widely publicized over the years that average actors are plutocrats, rolling in wealth, and that for them to seek to improve their working conditions is basest ingratitude. If this idea were founded on fact instead of on fiction, the Screen Actors Guild would never have been born." In 1933, when the Guild was formed, working conditions and pay were unregulated and oftentimes horrendous. Today, actors find protection from abuse both in pay and in working conditions, through the unions holding jurisdiction over particular kinds of performances. (Some of the standards and protections of the unions are discussed later in this chapter; other matters regarding conditions that may vary considerably in nonunion commercials and which the actor in those commercials must handle on his own are covered in Chapter 10.)

Any commercial or theatrical agent who isn't franchised by the appropriate union is not "legit." *Franchised* means that the agent has signed documents filed with the union stating that he will abide by the rules of the union; these rules state responsibilities and rights of both the agent and you the actor. In the Major Cities of New York, Los Angeles, and Chicago—and many other cities as well—nonfranchised agents cannot do anything for your career; legit commercial producers do *not* deal with nonfranchised agents.

SAG has jurisdiction over principal actors in TV shows, TV movies, educational and industrial films, feature films, and commercials which are shot on film. The Guild in New York, Boston, Philadelphia, Washington, D.C., and Baltimore negotiates and administers a contract covering extra players also—but not in any other city. The American Federation of Television and Radio Artists (AFTRA) has jurisdiction over performers in live and taped TV shows (newscasters and announcers included), taped commercials, radio shows, and phonograph records.

Since most commercials are shot on film in the larger cities, and since it is much easier to join AFTRA than SAG (as explained below), SAG is of much greater concern to the commercial actor in the larger cities than is AFTRA. Many agents will not interview you for possible representation if you're not a member of SAG. There is only one way to become eligible to join SAG: You must obtain a *principal* acting job from a producer who is shooting a union show with union contracts (whether SAG, AFTRA, or certain other performers' unions). Being an extra does not qualify you. The definition of a principal player in a commercial doesn't mean that one necessarily has to speak a line. (A principal player in *any other medium* must speak, or he is considered an extra, except for stage work where the actor might be an understudy for a larger role.)

A principal player in a commercial is anyone who is on camera and is identified with the product, demonstrates the product, or reacts to the message in the commercial. Also, a principal player is anyone who speaks a line on or off camera.

As you know by now, getting a principal role in a commercial is *no easy task*. My suggestion is to go ahead and start working on getting an agent, even if you're not in SAG. It will be harder to obtain one if you're not a member of that union, but keep trying. When you finally land an agent, hopefully he'll get you on interviews for SAG commercial acting jobs. Eventually, whether with your first agent or another, you'll walk in the door for a commercial interview and be so perfect for the job that you'll be hired. You will then be eligible to join SAG. Once you're a member, your agent will find it easier to get you into other commercial interviews.

You do not *have* to join SAG immediately. You can TAFT-HARTLEY your first job. "TAFT-HARTLEY" is a law stating that you can work a certain amount of time on a union job without having to join that union. Some of the unions interpret this law differently, but typically, as it applies to the acting unions, you can work up to thirty calendar days on your first job without joining the union. However, on any job that you obtain after thirty calendar days, or any job that continues over thirty calendar days, you must join if you want to work on a union show under that particular union. (This law does not apply to right-to-work states because a union cannot enforce mandatory membership in those states.)

Though you do not *have* to join immediately, I suggest doing so as soon as you're eligible. This will aid your agent, or your search for one, and will make you a more marketable product.

Agents aren't as concerned about your being a member of AFTRA as they are about your being a member of SAG, since (as mentioned earlier) it's easy to become a member of AFTRA and most commercials, at least in the larger markets, are shot on film. All you have to do to join AFTRA is pay the fees and dues. Therefore, being a member of AFTRA isn't as prestigious as being a member of SAG. If you are in one of the Major Cities, have the bucks and don't mind spending them, and are serious about being a professional actor, you might as well join AFTRA. Then you'll at least be a member of a professional acting union. But if you don't have the extra bucks, then it really isn't that important at this point. If you get a day's work under an AFTRA contract (excluding extra work), you can join SAG one year from the date you originally joined AFTRA. (For more details about joining the respective unions, contact their offices.)

As for joining the unions in the smaller markets, you must make that decision based on whether or not you want to become a professional actor, and how much union work is available in the town in which you plan to work. In other words, if there is an abundance of union work and less nonunion work, then you would definitely want to join. However, if there is very little union work and lots of nonunion work, you would have to decide whether to join and make more money per commercial with better working conditions, pension and welfare plans, etc., or perhaps work more, but for less money per commercial and without the benefits. Let me say this, however: if your goal is eventually to be a professional actor in a major market, I suggest that you consider joining SAG as soon as you are eligible and joining AFTRA as soon as it is advantageous to do so.

Extra players in *filmed* TV commercials come under the jurisdiction of the Screen Extras Guild (SEG) in Los Angeles, Las Vegas, San Francisco, Hawaii, and San Diego only; in New York, Boston, Philadelphia, Washington, D.C., and Baltimore, extra players come under the jurisdiction of SAG. There is no union covering extras in filmed commercials in other cities; they are usually just "picked up off the streets" in whatever city the commercial is being filmed. Extra players in *taped* TV commercials work under the jurisdiction of AFTRA, as do principal players. I do not suggest doing extra work in commercials in Los Angeles, if you want to be a professional principal actor in commercials. The idea that you start out as an extra and then move your way up went out with Ozzie and Harriet. What generally happens in Los Angeles is that commercial casting directors get to know you as an extra, and you might stay in that category (unfortunate, but true). As for doing extra work in cities other than Los Angeles, it probably could give you useful experience, but be sure to check with local people to determine the general attitude in your area.

Fees and Dues*

SAG—The initiation fee for joining SAG is $600, plus $37.50 for the first six months' dues; total joining fee is $637.50. Once you join, your dues payments vary depending on the amount of money you make under SAG and they are paid every six months.

AFTRA—The fees and dues vary from office to office. In Los Angeles the initiation fee is $600, plus $32.50 for the first six months' dues; total joining fee being $632.50. In New York the initiation fee is also $600, but the first six months' dues are $28.75; total joining fee being $628.75. As with SAG, once you've joined AFTRA your dues payments vary depending on the amount of money you make under AFTRA and they are also paid biannually.

Actor-Agency Contracts

Many actors *do not initially sign contracts* with an agent, even though the agent may agree to represent them. Sometimes agents feel that the paper work is not worth bothering with until you have your first job, or perhaps even until you have a major role. I was with my first agent (who represented me not only for commercials, but for all TV and film work) for four years before we ever signed a contract, and we only signed one at that time because I shot a pilot for a new TV series. For complete protection, the agent wanted me under contract in case the series ended up on the air, which it ultimately didn't.

If you're in a city where actors can freelance, then you have to make the decision whether or not to work exclusively under one

*These figures are accurate as this book goes to press in March 1984.

agent. In New York, for example, an actor can work under many agents *as long as he doesn't have a contract* with any of them; whoever gets that actor a particular job gets the commission for that job. In Los Angeles, however, it is against SAG rules to work under more than one agent for commercials, even if no contracts have been signed.

Whether you freelance or not, understand that verbal contracts should be considered ethically binding in this business! If an agent sends you on a commercial interview and you get the job, whether you are signed to that agent or not, you are *morally* obligated to pay him his ten percent. If you get a commercial acting job for yourself or through a third party (a very rare thing indeed) and you haven't signed a contract with the agent, then you are not morally obligated to pay him even though he may be working on your behalf for other interviews. I think it's a good idea to pay him anyway if he's been getting you out on interviews. The agent will probably work harder for you in the future if you're courteous; besides, he works for you many times without ever seeing a cent.

You can *sign contracts with only one agent at a time* for commercial representation. Obvious conflicts of interest would arise if two different *contracted* agents were pressing to get you into the same commercial interview.

The contracts you'll sign with a franchised agent are standard for each respective union. If an agent gives you the contracts (a set for SAG and/or a set for AFTRA) to sign while you're in his office, I suggest taking the time to look them over very thoroughly if you've never seen them. There's nothing in the SAG or AFTRA contracts that's tricky or anything along those lines, but you should always read over everything you sign. There is absolutely nothing wrong with taking the contracts home with you, if you want more time to look them over. Also, if you have any questions about a contract you can always check with the appropriate union for help. You'll sign three copies of each contract—one for you, one for your agent, and one for the appropriate union.

The contracts you sign with an agent guarantee the agent

that you'll give him ten percent of what you make from acting only, not, for instance, ten percent of your unemployment checks, even though he may be responsible for them. An agent is your representative and he deserves ten percent of what you make from any acting job you obtain while under his agency contract. After all, he works for you many times without getting paid, as pointed out earlier. He sends out your pictures and resumes and makes phone calls to casting personnel, and he doesn't get compensated unless you get the job. Of course, ANY COMMERCIAL OR THEATRICAL AGENT WHO CHARGES MORE THAN TEN PERCENT, OR CHARGES YOU ANY MONEY UP FRONT, ISN'T LEGIT BY INDUSTRY DEFINITION.

The agent may also ask you to sign check authorizations giving him permission to cash your checks from any acting employment. It's standard for an agent to do this; don't let it throw you. When an agent receives your check from a production company, he'll cash it at his bank and write you a check for your ninety percent of the original amount.

At this point, you might be wondering how you can protect yourself from being ripped off by your agent. Don't worry. First of all, before you start the job, you'll have to sign a contract for it, which clearly states your pay rate. Secondly, your agent will mail your statement of earnings from your employer with your check. Next, the union has a record of how much you made on the job; you can call its office if you have any problems. Lastly, you'll get your W-2 forms at the end of the year, stating your earnings. Quite frankly, I can't imagine, though it's possible, any franchised agent trying to rip you off. His entire business is at stake if he gets caught doing such a thing; he could be disenfranchised by the appropriate union, and there are too many ways for him to get caught.

Escape Clauses

The *original* SAG agency commercial contract you sign with a commercial agent only applies for a maximum of one year. (One year is standard though you could legally sign one for less.) SAG *renewal* agency contracts and AFTRA agency contracts with a commercial agent can be valid up to a maximum of three years. But these contracts don't necessarily bind you for the entire time of their jurisdiction.

If you've signed an *original* SAG agency commercial contract and you haven't made two thousand dollars or more in commercials in a period of 151 days, or have not had a "bona fide offer" of employment in the last 121 days, you can terminate the contract. ("Bona fide offer" means that the agent has secured an actual commercial acting job for you, contract and all, not just, for example, a submission of your photo and resume.) If you've signed a *renewal* SAG commercial contract with a commercial agent and you haven't made two thousand dollars or more in the last 91 days, you can release yourself from the contract. If you've signed an AFTRA commercial contract with a commercial agent and have worked fewer than 15 days in the last 91, you can release yourself from the contract.

Termination of any agency contract consists of writing a letter stating that you no longer wish to work with that agent, and sending a copy to the appropriate union(s) and one to the agent, and retaining a copy for your records. For more information regarding the dissolution of commercial agency contracts, contact the appropriate union(s).

Changing Agents

DON'T DROP YOUR "REGULAR" JOB WHEN YOU FIRST GET AN AGENT. It may take you a while to get established. All "established" really means is that you're able to make a living from acting. You will probably change agents many times in the course of your career. At times you'll feel that your agent isn't working for you. But keep in mind that it is extremely rare for an actor to make two thousand dollars in a 151-day period when he's just beginning. In the first 151 days don't expect to be so rich that when you cash a check, the bank will bounce.

Be careful about dumping an agent before you give him a chance to get you some interviews. The agent's job is to get you as many interviews as possible. His job is *not* actually to get you hired—that's your job. So, give the agent time.

If weeks go by and you haven't heard from your agent, simply phone him and ask why you haven't been sent on any interviews. Be courteous; he has a lot of clients to look after. Keep in mind that the fact that you're not going out on any interviews doesn't neceessarily mean that the agent isn't working for you. He may still be sending out your photos to commercial casting directors. It could be that you haven't really been "right" for any parts lately, or that your photos haven't been selling you, or whatever. This is why it's a good idea to contact your agent every few weeks to find out what's happening with your career.

When you phone your agent don't be belligerent or sarcastic. Saying things such as "I want to thank you for that last interview you sent me on . . . by the way, they have color in the movies now," isn't appropriate.

Should you decide that you could do better with another agent, don't dump the first agent until you have another one. It would be foolish to drop your only representative without having someone to take his place. You might find that no other agent is interested in you at that moment, and you should at least have some agent working on your behalf. On the other hand, there is nothing wrong with sending your photos and resumes out to other agents while you're being represented by the current one. It's done every day! Just keep in mind that dropping an agent, or having him drop you, is no fun. You then have to start all over again looking for another agent. Many actors are in this position continually. Changing agents ranks on my "preferability list" one notch above surgery.

Chapter Nine

The Commercial Interview

The typical way a commercial is cast is through personal contact: The casting director simply phones his agent friends and gives them descriptions of what types of characters he needs for a certain commercial. The agent then sends clients who fit those descriptions to the interview or submits photos of said clients, depending on what procedure that particular casting director likes to use.

An aid to casting which is increasingly being used is the service agency. Breakdown Services, Inc. is a theatrical (TV and film) communications network which creates and sends casting sheets by messenger to agents' offices in New York, London, and Los Angeles on a daily basis. Some commercials which are being cast in New York and London are listed on these sheets. In Los Angeles, Breakdown Services has a division for commercials called "Commercial Express." This office produces computer printouts in agents' offices, of casting information for the commercials being cast in the Los Angeles area. Another service in the Los Angeles area that utilizes computers for casting information is "Commercial Breakthru/In-Touch," which works in much the same way as "Commercial Express."

With the information from these service agencies, agents can submit photographs of their clients to the casting director of each commercial. The casting director looks through these photos and decides whom he wants to see on the interview. He then contacts the agents who represent those actors, and the agent, in turn, contacts those clients.

People casting commercials will sometimes, but rarely, have "open calls" where anyone can show up. Once in a blue moon the casting director has to look for a certain character that is hard to find. So he might put an ad in the acting trade papers, local newspapers, etc. These "cattle calls" get their name from the size of the crowds which show up. If you aren't from cow country, just imagine the exchange line at Macy's department store on December 26. Agents will rarely send actors on cattle calls for commercials in the major markets because they can usually set up personal appointments. In the smaller cities cattle calls are used more frequently, but still not very often.

Where Agents Don't Exist

In the smaller markets there might not be any union-franchised agents. In that case you might have to act as your own agent. You should submit your stapled pictures and resumes to local TV and radio stations, advertising agencies, any production houses in town, and even local merchants who use commercials on TV. You can let your fingers do the walking through the yellow pages to find such places. Some of the larger towns' telephone directories might contain the heading "Advertising—Television." If these folks don't produce the local commercials themselves (which most do), they can certainly direct you to the people who do.

Make follow-up phone calls a few days after your first contact. Since we're dealing with the smaller cities here, the people you talk to might not be doing any commercials at that particular moment, but you never know. The main thing is, you want them to keep your photos and resumes in their files for future use. See if you can set up an interview with the person(s) in charge of hiring the actors. A personal interview will improve your chances of being remembered in the future. Should you schedule an interview, you want to show the interviewer what a terrific personality you have, as I have discussed earlier.

Sometimes the local modeling/acting schools are contacted by the TV and radio stations or advertising agencies to send people to an interview. Will they represent you if you aren't enrolled in their school? That depends on the school. Most of them probably give better representation to their students even if they do represent outside talent. In defense of the modeling/acting schools, they do know their students' talents and abilities better than they do those of someone with whom they haven't worked.

Preparing for the Interview

As with any interview/audition, the commercial interview should not be dreaded. Quite the contrary. You should look upon it as an opportunity for employment; keep that foremost in your thoughts. You are going to be well prepared and organized, and you are going to be ready to *enjoy* the experience. Work on your attitude to really *like* the audition. Don't worry about whether the casting personnel like you—*you like them;* that you have control over. Besides, remember that they are not adversaries—they are on your side, they want you to do a good job. If you truly like the interview and the people in charge, you'll be giving off "positive vibes."

So when you finally do receive that phone call about an interview, you are going to be mentally prepared. Whoever calls you (agent, TV ad reps, modeling/acting school, etc.) will give you the pertinent information about the interview—where it is being held, who's casting, and for what product. He might give you a small indication of the character you'll be interviewing for, but many times he won't, especially in the major markets where an agent is very busy with many commercial casting calls.

I suggest that you get some kind of an appointment book to keep records of your interviews. You should write down the names (and job titles, if you know them) of the people whom you see. You can refer to these past interviews when going for another interview with the same people. Besides that, you'll need the records when income tax time comes around. The Screen Actors Guild has a terrific little calendar guide which anyone can purchase for a nominal fee. It's perfect for actors because it has sections to write down interview dates and locations, whom you saw, etc. You also need a good map of the city in which you plan to act in commercials. Interviews will be held all over town and it's really impossible to know all the streets in any city.

Commercials are cast very quickly. Many times your agent will call you the day of the interview! He may call you at noon to be at an interview by, say, one o'clock. This is why it's imperative for you to have an answering service. You should check your service for messages every hour! *You don't want to miss an interview just because you're too lazy to call in for messages.*

Beginning of the Interview

Be sure to bring copies of your photo and resume to the interview. Usually one set will be sufficient, but you should have another one with you just in case the interviewers want two copies of each. It is rare that they will, but sometimes the casting director and agencies both want a set.

You should arrive at the interview about fifteen to twenty minutes before your actual call-time, for two reasons: (1) it will give you time to look over the script, if there is one, and (2) you'll have a few minutes to relax and become familiar with the surroundings before you go into the interview.

We will assume for our purposes here that the interview is being held in the casting director's or ad agency's offices, which usually consist of a waiting room and a separate room for the actual interview. Let me point out, however, that I've been to commercial interviews which have taken place in everything from a hotel room to a street corner. These are not the norm, though. The hotel room was used because the client was from out of town and staying at that hotel, and the street corner was used because the commercial was to be shot on that same street corner and the casting personnel wanted to see how we "fit in" on that corner.

The interview really starts as soon as you enter the reception room, so start being friendly and kind the minute you walk in. The first person you see might be a secretary. Be nice to the secretary— just as the agents' secretaries of today may be future agents, casting directors' secretaries of today may be the casting directors of tomorrow! Also, the casting director for this interview will be coming in and out of the reception room calling actors into the interview, and he will be seeing your behavior. The positive vibes should begin right away.

You'll register on the "sign-in" sheet. Write your name, your agent's name, your social security number, and the time you arrived.

While at the interview, you must be very careful not to make value judgments about the dialogue of the commercial. Let's face it: commercial dialogue is sometimes very stilted and hard to deliver because it sounds so ridiculous. Many actors sit around in the reception room talking about how they really don't want to be on commercial interviews. But *you* are going to be professional enough to realize that if they really didn't want to be on the interview, they wouldn't be there. And their negative attitude can't help but hurt their performances when they get into the actual interview. Whatever you do, don't give the casting personnel the impression that you think you are lowering yourself by being in a commercial. If Laurence Olivier and Bob Hope can do commercials, then so can you. Keep a warm, positive attitude about the entire commercial from the moment you walk into the reception room to the moment you leave the interview.

Pay no attention to all the self-serving egotistical actors who will be talking about all their credits. On interviews actors love to see other actors with whom they've worked so they can talk about the show they did together and let the other actors know they were once working. Forget the nonsense. The actors who work the most are often the most silent about their credits. No matter what they say, realize that half the actors at the interview eat at McDonald's, and the other half work there.

Actors make fools of themselves by trying to impress the other auditioners. For example, once I was on an interview and this young lady sitting next to me in the reception room was reading *HOW TO ACT & EAT AT THE SAME TIME*. I wanted a true reaction from her about my book, so I told her how many bad things I had heard about it. She disagreed, and said how much she was enjoying reading it. I then looked over the Table of Contents of the book and remarked that I just couldn't see any valuable information in it. She turned to me with a look that could kill and said, "Listen . . . kid . . . Tom Logan, the author, happens to be a very close friend of mine and I don't think he'd appreciate you saying those things." She was a little embarrassed when the casting director came into the reception room and called out the next interviewee, "Tom Logan." I was flattered that she defended my book and I subsequently thanked her—but don't embarrass yourself with such attempts at one-upmanship. Instead, look over your script if there is one, and if not, spend the time relaxing or engaging in pleasant conversation.

And forget trying to size up the other actors. Suppose, for example, you feel out of place because they all look alike and you look completely different. This makes you stand out. True, since everyone else looks alike, they are probably the type that is being sought. But you never know, so don't let self-doubt ruin your performance.

That problem came up when I was interviewing for a Coppertone commercial. Everyone I saw in the reception room was big and brawny. I felt so out of place; I mean better bodies than mine can be seen in used-car lots. Obviously my agent had made a mistake in sending me to the interview. (This happens sometimes, so be prepared for it.) Instead of letting this work against me, however, I decided I would go in and act like a complete weakling. I mean, what did I have to lose? Up against all of the other interviewees, I did look like a weakling anyway, and I always think you should leave the interview with the people in charge remembering you. Anyway, to make a long story short, I acted like a complete wimp. They changed the commercial around because they liked the character I presented. I got the job because I let the handicap (not fitting the physical type they wanted originally) be a plus. This won't usually work, of course, but the point is, always do your best and make an impression. *Remember: You're not only interviewing for one job, but also for any other jobs these same people might be casting in the future.*

Before the Screen Test

When you interview for a commercial, usually you'll say your lines from Q-cards or from the script—that is, if there is any planned dialogue for you to say. Since you often won't know if there is planned dialogue or not, you should arrive early, as I suggested at the beginning of this chapter. If the script is available, you'll want time to look it over. Even if cue cards are to be used in the screen test, casting directors usually will have the script available in the lobby. Do study the script, although you will use the Q-cards, if they are available, on the actual screen test. (If cue cards *are* to be used, be sure to read them before you start shooting the screen test. The words on the Q-cards may be slightly different from those of the script you read in the reception room or lobby. For some reason, when changes are made, they aren't always marked in both the script and the Q-cards.) If no planned dialogue is to be used, then you'll have a few minutes just to relax.

If there is more than one part you could possibly play, be sure to look over all those parts very carefully. When you get into the interview, you might be asked to play all the parts you are "right for."

If you are to be working with a partner, sometimes the casting director will tell you who your partner is before you enter the interview. If you're lucky enough to find out this information beforehand, I strongly suggest your getting together with that partner, going outside, and working together speaking the lines *out loud*. That way you can *work off of each other* and there will be no surprises during the interview. Be sure to let the other interviewees know where you are in case your names are called before you step back inside the lobby. *Don't go too far!* In fact, just step right outside the door. The worst thing you can do is to be absent when your name is called.

Even if you aren't told with whom you are going to be working, I suggest taking a partner and working with him. This will give you practice playing off of someone, even though he might not be the person you'll actually be interviewing with. If you're the only person to be speaking in the commercial, it still will do you a lot of good to step just outside the door and say the lines in the commercial out loud.

You might even have time to memorize the script before the screen test. *But don't take chances.* Even if you *do* memorize it with your photographic memory, you might forget to take the lens cap off, so take the script into the interview with you unless otherwise instructed (as in the case where cue cards are to be used for the screen test). Under pressure you might be nervous and need to refer to it. That's okay. The interviewers are not running a memory contest; they just want to see that you can perform the material. Your stopping in the middle of your performance because you can't remember a line only interrupts the interview. Better to be safe than sorry!

Also, there's a psychological reason for not letting them think you have memorized the commercial: it appears as though you are giving a performance, not an audition. This being the case, they think that your "performance" won't improve very much. However, if you are giving a cold reading, they realize that you'll be working on your performance and by the time the commercial is actually shot you'll give a better one. Even if you know it completely by heart, I'm not so sure it's a good idea to let them know that. Whether you agree or not, it's definitely something to think about.

Do learn, however, the *first and last sentences* of your lines. You wouldn't want to greet someone while looking away from him. If you start performing the commercial while looking away from the lens (and if you're supposed to be speaking to the audience), you aren't making the best first impression; you seem less warm and sincere from the very start. Surely you can learn the first few words, if not the whole first sentence, and thus keep your eyes off the script when you begin the commercial. By the same token, you wouldn't want to say good-bye to someone while looking the other way. So, grasp the words in the first and last sentences, if nothing else!

Usually the casting director will come out into the lobby and call the actors into the screen test, as mentioned earlier. Don't forget your photo and resume (many actors spend their time in the lobby passing them around). Remember to have a backup photo and resume in case they want two.

It's really hard to say who will be in the interview. Usually it will be one person (the cameraman) or a small group. I'll be using the term "the group" to designate the casting director, cameraman, ad agency rep, director, producer, and product representative, or a combination thereof. Rarely will this many people ever be in the interview.

When you walk in, be calm. Try to act confident (as I have stressed earlier). You don't want to give the impression that you are "green." You should realize that if you come across like that in the interview, the group will be worried that you'll come across that way to the public—which would be a killer for their product.

Relax and be friendly. A firm handshake and a smile when you walk in can help to set a positive tone. If you sense tension in the room, try to lighten the mood, but be yourself—don't try to alter your personality to fit what you think others expect of you.

And, if in the course of the interview you make a fool of yourself, too bad, but have a good time anyway. Show that you are professional enough to handle a difficult situation with grace and humor. Even if you don't get this job, you will leave a good impression with the interviewers for the *next time.*

The group may have a very short chitchat session with you to get an idea of your personality and how it relates to the character(s) in the commercial. If only the cameraman is present, he can probably give you some information about the commercial. If there is a chitchat session for the sole purpose of getting to know you, it's fine to hold a conversation, but don't be long-winded—these people don't have all day!

Someone in the interview will give you instructions about what they're looking for. As you listen to these instructions, *be very attentive!* The interviewer might be the person who will decide whether to hire you, and even if he isn't, he probably received his instructions from the person(s) who will make that decision. Once they have given you their interpretation of the character, it's your turn to interpret what they have said in your performance.

The Screen Test

Now they'll start to "roll" the camera. When the cameraman gives you your cue, you will "slate." This means that you will state your name, and unless otherwise instructed, also that of your agent. Smile when you say your name. After all, this is the first thing the group will see you perform. Be understood when you say your name. It's also a good idea to say, "Hi, I'm _____." The extra "hi" or "hello" gives your performance a nice friendly touch.

Pause after you slate, before you actually start performing the commercial. You don't want to run them together; you want your name to stand out and not be garbled into the commercial.

GO FOR SOME KIND OF CHARACTER—BUT BE

YOURSELF, NOT AN "ACTOR." Do something different so that you'll be remembered. Say the dialogue with a unique twist or whatever. Most people can forgive a bad performance, but not a boring one. Keep in mind that the group may be sitting through literally hundreds of actors reciting the same dialogue. It's very refreshing when someone comes along and tries something different; that person will probably be on the call back.

IF YOU SCREW UP, RECOVER AND GO ON. Suppose you begin the screen test and just about three lines into the dialogue you mess up a line. What do you do? Smile, smirk, laugh, or cover your face with your hands? Perhaps you should say "cut," and stop your performance. NO, to all of the above. One of the amateur's biggest problems is stopping before he hears the word "cut" from the director. (This is especially true when you're finally on the set shooting the commercial. No matter how bad you think a particular "take" is when shooting an actual commercial, continue until you are told to stop. You never know, your best take may be the one you goofed up. Perhaps it made the commercial look much more "human" and natural. Even if a particular take looks bad during an actual shooting, the editor can sometimes cut around a mistake and save an otherwise good take.)

I guess if you flub the first line on the interview, it probably wouldn't be a disaster just to start over. However, if you can regain composure and go on, do so. When you're a few lines into the script and you mess up a line, it's a bad policy to express all kinds of negative reactions to it. Saying things like, "Wait," or "Uh . . . uh . . . uh . . ." isn't a good representation of your work. Becoming hysterical because you messed up a line is only going to convince your interviewers that you are an amateur. If you act like nothing happened and just continue, it shows them that you have composure and won't come completely unglued during the actual shooting should you be cast.

There is absolutely nothing wrong with making a goof while performing the commercial in the interview. It happens to everyone many times in his career, and it will not keep you from being cast in the commercial. The group realize that you are looking at the script for the first time and that you'll have time to work on your delivery if you are cast in the commercial. What they are looking for are people who look and act professional and have an air of confidence about them. They aren't necessarily looking for people who, in one chance, can get all the way through the dialogue without a mistake. Of course you look better if your performance is smooth, but there have been many interviews where I have screwed up a line or two, and ended up being cast in the commercial.

PAUSE BEFORE WALKING OFF. Many actors walk off camera when they get through saying the script during the screen test. They don't realize that the cameraman will probably "hold" the camera on their faces for a few seconds after they get through. This is done to give the casting personnel a better idea of how well the actors "photograph." Be sure you hear the camera cut off before you walk off frame. Otherwise, since the camera is probably focused tightly on your face, it will appear as though you are running off camera. A speaker should not leave the podium as he is finishing his last words; neither should you walk off camera before a good long pause.

After you have performed the commercial once, the group will probably excuse you. In some cases, however, they may want you to do it again. Also, if you want to try it a different way, there's nothing wrong with asking them if you can do it over again after you have completely finished one take; just realize that there might not be enough time to do so. Whatever you do, don't ask to see the videotape playback. There usually isn't enough time to show it to you. If the cameraman were to show every actor's audition back to him, the readings would take twice as much time.

After the Screen Test

Whether you are asked to read again or not is no indication of the quality of your performance. You could have been so terrific on the first reading that that's all the casting personnel need to see; or you could have been so wrong for the part that they've seen enough. Or, it could be that they liked you enough to give you another chance to try the commercial with a different slant. Or, it could be that physically you are so right for the part that they want to give you another chance, even though your first reading was less than adequate. In other words, you can't figure them out, so don't try!

The group will excuse you by saying something like, "Thank you for coming in." Thank them back, and scoot. Don't make it hard for them to get you out the door. Keep in mind that they are probably watching you as you leave, so maintain the smile and good posture.

Back in the reception room, you'll sign out on the "sign-in" sheet. The main reason for this record, on union commercials, is for proof to SAG or AFTRA (depending on whether the commercial is shot on film or tape, respectively) of how long you were kept at the interview. (Union regulations regarding payment for duration and number of interviews are explained in Chapter 10.)

When you leave the audition, forget about it! You really don't know what they want in the character or physical type, so don't ponder for days upon days trying to figure it out. If you get a call back, great, but don't brood over the interview once you've left it.

—The Call Backs

Not all commercial interviews include any call backs, but many do. Basically the call back works the same way as the original interview. Unless otherwise instructed, you should dress and act the same way you did on the original interview. Obviously, if they are calling you back they are interested in the way you presented yourself on the first interview.

After the Interview

I think it's extremely important to write a thank-you note to the casting director of the commercial. You might not have seen the casting director while you were on the interview, but he is the one responsible for your being there. If there is no casting director involved then you should write to the person with whom you had contact during the interview. A nice handwritten note thanking the person for interviewing you and mentioning that you hope he will keep you in mind for the future is standard. Thank-you notes can never hurt you. Just remember to keep them short because the people you'll be writing to are very busy.

If you're cast in the commercial, you'll be notified through your agent if you have one, and directly if you don't. Keep in mind that if you're not cast that doesn't necessarily mean that whoever was in charge didn't like you or your acting. Remember that you simply might not be the best type for the job, or that they might have been "matching" people for the commercial. For instance, let's say they were looking for a family which consists of beautiful people. But let's suppose you look like Grant—General, not Cary. Obviously, you wouldn't be what they were looking for physically. It really wouldn't matter how terrific your reading was, you probably wouldn't get the part. Also, remember that as many as hundreds of people were probably seen for that commercial, so your odds are low. But don't be discourged; think of each audition as a learning experience in preparation for future opportunities. Just keep going on interviews and one day you'll be right for a part. It's a numbers game!

Chapter Ten

Pay and Working Conditions

One of the greatest aspects of performing in commercials is the pay. In this chapter I will give you some ideas about what you can possibly get paid for performing in a commercial. And I'll describe working conditions, so that when you go to shoot your first commercial, you won't feel so "out of it."

Before getting into the specifics, I'd like to mention some general comments about working on the job. First of all, be sure to arrive early for the shooting of your commercial. DON'T BE LATE. This seems obvious enough, but I cannot tell you how many times I've sat around on sets waiting for lazy actors to show up for work. It's extremely unprofessional to be late! You are costing the production company mucho bucks, wasting everyone's time, and showing what an amateur you are.

Another important rule is to be nice to everyone on the set. This includes *everybody*—makeup personnel, lighting people, and anyone else on the set. Even if you don't agree with me that you should be courteous to these people because as a human being you should treat people well, you can see that these are the people who are going to make you look good in the commercial; they are there to help you, so be cooperative. Besides, you never know what people might be doing in the future.

As an example, take my experience a few years back when I

was working in a movie called MASSACRE AT CENTRAL HIGH. None of the extras had dressing rooms and they were left out in the cold. I let them use my dressing room, but many of the other actors couldn't be bothered with them. In fact, one actor, who shall remain unnamed, was downright rude to them. It just so happens that one of the extras in that movie is now a top Hollywood screenwriter; we often visit, sometimes talking about the actors from that picture with whom he refuses to work. Bottom line: Be the type of person who is liked *wherever* he goes, not *whenever* he goes.

Union Commercials

The following information concerning pay and working conditions is a thumbnail sketch of the SAG and AFTRA commercial contracts. (The SAG and AFTRA commercial contracts were negotiated in parity, so the payments are the same for both unions.) The working conditions described here by no means comprise an exhaustive list, but these are the more common ones you will be working under. Note that the basic pay figures here will increase when the new SAG and AFTRA commercial contracts are negotiated in 1985. If you're shooting a nonunion commercial, these figures and requirements do not apply; see the section on nonunion commercials later in this chapter.

Basic Pay

Who keeps track of how many interviews you had and how many times your commercial airs? Who calculates how much you are owed for these airings? Sit down and relax; the people who scheduled you for the interview(s) and hired you for the commercial—the advertising agency—keep track of how much money you are owed.

You're probably thinking how easy it would be for them to cheat you out of your money. Don't worry. If your commercial plays more times than the advertising agency has logged, the ad agency must pay the TV station or network for the air time out of its own pocket; the agency won't get reimbursed by the client for airings not recorded in the books. Therefore the ad agency is going to be careful to show accurately how many times the commercial has aired. Sometimes a commercial might air in an area by accident when some local TV man throws it on at the last minute. The ad agency will still get billed by the TV station, and you, in turn, will get paid. Usually if there's a mistake, it's just that—a mistake. But mistakes are the exception rather than the rule.

Interviews

You will receive no payment for the first hour of the initial interview or the first call back. But if you are kept over an hour on either of these, you will be paid $19.84 per half hour after the first hour, with fractions of a half hour rounded in your favor. For example, if you're on the interview or first call back for an hour and three minutes, you'll be paid $19.84; if you're there for an hour and thirty-five minutes, you'll be paid $39.68; and so on. Because of these overtime payments, you'll rarely be kept over an hour. You'll receive these payments whether or not you're in SAG or AFTRA, as long as the commercial is under jurisdiction of one of these contracts.

If you are called back a second time (third interview), you'll be paid $79.35 for any time under two hours. If you're called back a third time (fourth interview), you'll be paid $158.70 for any time under four hours. For any time over two hours on the third interview or for any time over four hours on the fourth interview, the same payment plan per half hour described earlier is used for the remaining time (i.e., $19.84 per half hour or fraction thereof). Because of these payments, you'll rarely have three interviews for a union commercial acting job. For nonunion commercials, you will most likely never get paid for interviewing.

Commercials

If the commercial is under the jurisdiction of SAG or AFTRA, you will be paid a "session fee" for the day's work, whether the commercial eventually airs or not. You will be paid a minimum of $317.40 per commercial per shooting day. In other words, if you work two days on one commercial, you will be paid two session fees, and if you shoot two commercials in one day, you will be paid two session fees even though you only shoot one day. If the commercial does not end up on the air, and many of them don't, that is all you will be paid, unless you have some overtime or wore your own clothes. There are small fees here and there, but the basic pay is your session fee.

Your payments for airings will depend on the "usage" of the particular advertisement. Usage of commercials falls under many classifications, definitely too many to mention here. We'll discuss the two most common ones—Class A Program Use and Wild Spots.

Class A Program Use means that the commercial airs in over twenty cities as part of the network broadcast of a particular program. If you were in a commercial which aired Class A, you would make the following minimum amounts per airing: second airing, $122.68; third through thirteenth airing, $97.34; fourteenth and thereafter, $46.66. (There is no payment for the first airing as that is part of your sesson fee.)

Wild Spot usage means that you are paid by market, instead of per airing, and that the commercial is broadcast by local stations. The payments depend on the number of markets and the number of people in those markets that broadcast the commercial. For this type of commercial, the performer receives a one-time fee based on the number of markets and population of those markets for every thirteen weeks that the commercial airs, no matter how many times it airs in those thirteen weeks.

Product Conflict

When you shoot a commercial under the jurisdiction of SAG or AFTRA, you will have to sign a form stating that you will not be in any commercial whose product "conflicts" (competes) with the original product you are endorsing. You are being "held" to that original commercial until it stops airing and/or the advertiser releases you from the contract. An advertiser can hold you to a certain commercial for the amount of time specified in the contract. You will receive a "holding fee" every thirteen weeks for which you are being held. The holding fee is equal to your session fee (your daily rate for the shooting of that commercial).

Wardrobe

It is likely that for a commercial you'll have a wardrobe fitting. This is especially true when you have to wear certain outfits. For instance, if you were performing in a McDonald's commercial as a counter person, you would most likely have to be fitted for the company uniform that counter persons wear in their commercials. Even in cases where you aren't required to wear a certain outfit for a certain company, it is not uncommon that they will fit you into regular clothes—football jersey, jogging outfit, etc.

You will be paid $39.68 for the first hour of the fitting. (The advertising agency has to pay you for a full hour even if you're only there for one minute.) You are then paid $39.68 for each additional hour, in fifteen-minute increments. Each fifteen-minute increment is compenstated by one-fourth of the $39.68.

If you use your own clothes during the shooting, you'll be paid $10 for each outfit which is non-evening (informal) wear. For evening (formal) wear, you'll be paid $20 per outfit. If you are required to purchase an outfit (which is rare), then be sure to keep the receipts. You will be reimbursed for such a purchase.

Meals

The producer of the commercial is required to feed you, or to give you time to eat, at certain times of the day, or pay a substantial penalty for starving you. He must feed you your first meal within five and a half hours of your original call-time. For the first half hour over that time (or any fraction thereof), you will be paid $25. The second half hour is also $25. For the third half hour and each subsequent half hour, you will receive $50 per half hour.

You must be fed the second meal within six hours from the time you finished your first meal. The meal penalty payments for the second meal are the same as for the first. Meal requirements on location shooting are described below.

In some instances it saves the producer money to keep shooting when you are supposed to be given time to eat. Perhaps the sun is going down, for example, and if they don't finish shooting, the production company will have to go into another day's shooting, which will end up costing the producer much more money than he would pay in meal penalties.

Location Shooting

Location shooting is any shooting that is not at the studio. You are paid for driving from the studio if you have to provide your own transportation to a spot within the "studio zone," which means any location within a certain number of miles from a certain point in the city. In Los Angeles, for example, any location within thirty miles, as the crow flies, from the corner of La Cienega and Beverly Boulevard is considered within the studio zone. If you are traveling to a local location, you are paid twenty cents for each mile from the studio. If you happen to live next door to the location, but twenty-five miles from the studio, for instance, you will still be paid twenty cents per mile from the studio. It also works in the reverse, however; if you live far away from the location which happens to be two miles from the studio, for instance, you will only be paid for the two miles.

If travel is to a location outside of the studio zone, the producer must provide your transportation, and the time you are picked up begins your workday. SAG and AFTRA require that you have "first class" transportation—usually defined as air transportation if it is available. However, the travel could be by limousine if it's a short distance (i.e., a few hours).

If the shooting is out of town and you travel to an overnight location on a day when you are not actually performing, you are paid for a full day if you leave before noon. If you leave between noon and six o'clock in the evening, you are paid for a half day. If you leave after 6 P.M., you are paid for each hour of travel at $39.68 in hourly increments. On any overnight location the producer must pay for the actor's lodging, which is defined as "reasonable" lodging in the SAG and AFTRA contracts. In other words, staying at such places as the "No-Tell Motel" would be questionable, unless there were no other lodging available nearby.

While on any overnight location, you must be paid a "per diem" (per day fee) for meals. The total per diem for food is $44.44. This breaks down into $8.46 for breakfast, $12.70 for lunch, and $23.28 for dinner. Instead of paying you cash for food, the producer can feed you at his expense. Be forewarned: location food isn't always the best; you might prefer Kal Kan or Top Choice.

Rest Periods Between Days

Actors should avoid being tired. We don't look our best or do our best work when we've been without sleep. Unfortunately, shooting days are usually long and very tiring. To avoid having you work too many days in a row without adequate rest, under the SAG and AFTRA contracts, the producer (with a few exceptions) must pay a penalty if you don't have twelve hours off from the time you leave one day until the time you are called for the next day's work. You will receive a full day's pay for any "forced call," up to a maximum of $500.

Overtime, Saturdays, Sundays, and Holidays

If you work "overtime," i.e., beyond the basic eight hours in one weekday for a single "session," you will be paid time and a half for the ninth and tenth hours, and double time in units of one hour for time over ten hours.

Producers are allowed to work you on Saturdays and Sundays, but they must pay a premium for doing so. If you're making double scale or less, you will be paid double for each of these days; if you're making more than double scale, you will be paid time and a half of your daily rate. Producers are also permitted to work you on holidays, but must pay you double your daily rate, no matter what your daily rate is. The overtime payments for the above days are figured the same was as they would be if you were shooting on a weekday.

Nonunion Commercials

When dealing with nonunion commercials you aren't as protected as you are with union productions. Therefore, you will have to do a little investigating on your own. For instance, you won't be signing standard SAG or AFTRA agreements with the producer(s) of the commercial. Read your contract over very carefully and consult with an attorney if you have *any* legal questions about it whatsoever. What are your legal rights? How long can the producer run the commercial? What about insurance? Are you covered in the event that you get hurt while shooting their commercial? The legal questions go on and on, so be sure that you understand them.

There are also many nonlegal areas you should check out. Are you going to be paid for mileage to and from the studio if the shooting is on location? Will you be paid overtime for the shooting? What if the commercial takes two days to shoot and you were only contracted for one? Will you get paid for the extra day? What about wardrobe? If you use your own, will you be paid extra? If you are required to purchase an outfit, is the producer going to reimburse you? Are you supposed to wear your own makeup? If so, check beforehand to see exactly what the director wants concerning makeup—how much, what type, etc. I'm not implying that the producer should or should not pay you extra for this or that. I'm only pointing out that there are many things you should check out *before the shooting*. And, you *might* be able to negotiate extra payments for some things in your contract, by being well informed ahead of time.

Also, by checking things beforehand, you may be able to avoid abuses in employment which could take place on a nonunion set. Besides possible abuses related to the various matters mentioned above, you'll have no union to protect you from safety hazards and to enforce regulations regarding minors. Hopefully, the producer will follow the state labor laws of whichever state you're working in, but you won't have SAG or AFTRA looking over his shoulder.

In many of the smaller markets, you will be performing all tasks—you may be actor, wardrobe person, makeup artist, etc. It's very doubtful that you'll receive any use fees (i.e., residuals) or payments for interviews, wardrobe calls, etc. For most local commercials shot in local areas, you'll probably receive a "buy out." This means that you'll be paid a flat sum for performing in the commercial. Under the "buy out," you'll receive no more money for the commercial after your original payment, no matter how many times, or where, it airs.

Though the money in the smaller markets will not add up as it does in the national markets, be happy that you were cast. After all, you'll probably be paid something for the commercial; you'll get great experience; you'll probably have a wonderful time; and finally, but not least importantly, you'll get to see your face on the "tube."

Finale

People sometimes look at me very strangely when I say that there are many, many actors who make their living exclusively from acting in commercials. Some of them make a terrific living for only a few days work every year. But before you dream about laughing all the way to the bank (and then buying it), or about the Jones' keeping up with you . . . keep reading. You are entering an area of the acting profession which is, contrary to public opinion, one of the most difficult. It's a tough, competitive business. Some actors have been out of work so long that they're getting gold watches from the unemployment office. And, since most actors are constantly broke, they have to have other jobs besides acting: tending bar, driving cabs, selling furniture (their own), etc.

The statistics from the Screen Actors Guild (the union having jurisdiction over actors with regard to performances shot on film) are horrifying. The 1982 figures for income earned under SAG jurisdiction are as follows:

> 57% of the members earned less than $1,000 annually;
> 81.5% earned less than $5,000 annually;
> 88.5% earned less than $10,000 annually;
> 94.7 earned less than $25,000 annually;
> only 2.6% earned more than $50,000 annually.

That's the bad news. The good news is that SAG members made a total of $230,788,256 in TV commercials, which is more than they made in television programs and movies *combined.* (The figure for TV shows is $170,798,860; for movies, $54,604,086.)

These figures don't take into account all of the local actors across the country who are making nonunion commercials. Though a large majority of *national* commercials are made in the Major Cities of Hollywood, Chicago, and New York, literally thousands of commercials are made annually in cities all across the U.S.

To take advantage of these employment opportunities, the beginning commercial actor must overcome many obstacles. First, you must get a wonderful head shot. Second, you need a nice resume. Third, a good agent. But managing these acts isn't as difficult as the finale—actually getting the commercial job. You'll go on interview after interview without landing a role. Commercial producers see hundreds upon hundreds of actors for each commercial. Many times you'll feel like a fugitive from the law of averages. Please believe me when I say that every actor has felt this way at some time in his career, and many are feeling that way right this minute; so don't give up!

Chapter 10 outlined *minimum* payments for principal actors in TV commercials under union auspices. As you gain experience, commercial acting may pay you *very* well indeed. However, while looking for that break into the commercial acting field, you'll need money to survive—unless you're lucky enough to have had some rich uncle leave you an inheritance. If you want to be a professional actor, money won't bring you happiness, but it will keep you comfortable while you're unhappy. So get a steady job that will allow you to leave for interviews.

To many actors, commercials are the end goal. Many completely unknown actors have been thrown into the star limelight for their commercial work. To other actors, commercials are a great way to make some bucks on the side while trying to get a break into episodic TV or feature films. There is only one way to be successful in the acting profession, be it commercials, TV, film, or stage—and that is by the age-old formula of persistance. I do truly believe that one can accomplish whatever he wants if he is willing to work for it. Apply the techniques in my book that you like, discard the ones that don't suit you, and invent your own to fit your personality. With the addition of a little luck, you may see yourself in one of those million-dollar minutes on national TV.

Appendices

Appendix A

Commercial Scripts for Practice

These scripts can be useful to you for both (a) familiarizing yourself with the terms defined in Chapter 2 as they are used in actual commercial scripts and (b) practicing techniques you learned from Chapters 3, 4, and 5.

The Leo Burnett Company, one of the major advertising firms in the country, kindly furnished these scripts, which were designed for their clients The Kellogg Company and the Procter & Gamble Company, as indicated. Actual scripts like these are typed in columns on 8½ " × 11 " paper. My presentation in this book uses two facing pages because of the space restrictions. Otherwise, it follows as closely as possible the original scripts.

In the AUDIO portion of the Kellogg Company scripts, underlining indicates trademark for the purpose of this book. In the Procter & Gamble Company scripts, underlining appears in the originals to indicate emphasis.

LEO BURNETT U.S.A.

KELLOGG COMPANY
30-Second Film
"STORE"
PRODUCT 19

<u>VIDEO</u>

1 INT. HOMEY "MA AND PA" GROCERY.
   PERNELL ROBERTS WALKING INTO
   FRAME UP TO CEREAL SECTION.

2 HE PICKS UP A BOX OF PRODUCT 19.

3 CUT TO CU 100% GRAPHICS ON BOX.

4 CUT TO MCU ROBERTS WITH CEREAL.

5 CAMERA STAYS WITH HIM AS HE
   CONTINUES TO WALK.

6 CAMERA TIGHTENS.

7 ROBERTS TAPS KELLOGG'S LOGO
   ON BOX.

8 CUT TO BEAUTY SHOT OF BOX AND
   BOWL. SUPER: "HIGH NUTRITION FROM
   KELLOGG'S." "© 1982 KELLOGG COMPANY."

PRUDENTIAL PLAZA • CHICAGO, ILLINOIS 60601
TELEPHONE: (312) 565-5959

As Filmed and Recorded: 07/06/82   rj

AUDIO

PERNELL: It can boggle the mind trying to
pick a high nutrition cereal.

Kellogg's® Product 19®

has one hundred percent of a whole
day's allowance of nine vitamins and iron.

And so does another cereal. Product 19's
a little different.

It's the only one of those cereals that's
made from four wholesome grains.

Corn, oats, wheat and rice.
Gettin' easier to pick, isn't it?

And Kellogg's has something else.
Kellogg's has Kellogg's...

ANNCR: (VO) And that's quality. High
nutrition from four grains and Kellogg's.

LEO BURNETT U.S.A.

KELLOGG COMPANY
30-Second Film
"WHAT'S IN IT FOR YOU?"
PRODUCT 19

VIDEO

1   OPEN ON ECU OF PERNELL SITTING ON
   HIS FRONT PORCH.

2   SHOT WIDENS.

3   CUT TO CU PRODUCT 19 AND TOTAL
   PACKAGES. PERNELL PICKS UP PRODUCT 19.

4   PERNELL POURS PRODUCT 19 INTO BOWL.

5   ECU SPOONING PRODUCT 19.

6   PERNELL WITH SPOONFUL OF PRODUCT 19 AND
   THE PRODUCT 19 PACKAGE.

7   PULL BACK. PERNELL WITH PRODUCT 19 PACKAGE
   AND BOWL OF CEREAL.

PRUDENTIAL PLAZA • CHICAGO, ILLINOIS 60601
TELEPHONE: (312) 565-5959

Approved for Bidding: 10/28/82 rj
Revision #1: 11/02/82 rj
Revision #2: 11/23/82 rj

AUDIO

PERNELL: If you eat a high nutrition cereal

because of what's in it for you,
maybe you should know more about
what's in it. Does it have one
hundred percent of nine vitamins
and iron?

These do. And four wholesome grains?

Only <u>Product 19</u>® does. That's
why it's my cereal.

It has corn, oats, wheat and rice.

And there's something else in it
for me...

<u>Kellogg's</u>®.

LEO BURNETT U.S.A.

VIDEO

8   ECU PERNELL.

9   ECU PRODUCT 19 PACKAGE ON PORCH WITH SUPER:
    "THE HIGH NUTRITION CEREAL FROM KELLOGG'S."
    SUPER: "©1982 KELLOGG COMPANY."

PRUDENTIAL PLAZA • CHICAGO, ILLINOIS 60601
TELEPHONE: (312) 565-5959

AUDIO

Shouldn't that be the one you're
eating?

ANNCR: (VO) <u>Product 19</u>. The high nutrition
cereal from <u>Kellogg's</u>.

LEO BURNETT U.S.A.

KELLOGG COMPANY
30-Second Film
"FUN TO EAT/FARMER-ADULT"
MINI WHEATS

<u>VIDEO</u>

1 FARMER WITH BOX IN FIELD OF WHEAT.

2 KIDS POP UP.

3 MOM IN KITCHEN.

4 KIDS POP UP.

5 2 PKG. SHOT WITH COMPLETE
   BREAKFAST.

6 FOOTBALL COACH.

PRUDENTIAL PLAZA • CHICAGO, ILLINOIS 60601
TELEPHONE: (312) 565-5959

Approved for Bidding: 12/02/81 pm
Revision #3: 01/04/82 pm
Revision #4: 01/12/82 pm

AUDIO

FARMER: Whole grain wheat helps make
          Kellogg's® Mini-Wheats® very nutritious.

CHORUS   AND IT REALLY, REALLY, REALLY, TASTES
KIDS: DELICIOUS!

MOM: Kellogg's Frosted Mini-Wheats® is a
          shredded wheat cereal that's good
          for you.

CHORUS   AND IT REALLY, REALLY, REALLY, TASTES
KIDS: GOOD TOO!

ANNCR: Kellogg's Frosted and Apple Frosted
          Mini-Wheats® cereals--little biscuits
          lightly sweet made of crunchy
          wheat..

COACH: Kellogg's Frosted Mini-Wheats has the
          nutrients of whole grain wheat.

LEO BURNETT U.S.A.

VIDEO

7 KIDS POP UP.

8 PKG. SHOT SUPER: "SHREDDED WHEAT
   THAT'S FUN TO EAT." SUPER: " ©
   1982 KELLOGG COMPANY."

PRUDENTIAL PLAZA • CHICAGO, ILLINOIS 60601
TELEPHONE: (312) 565-5959

AUDIO

CHORUS KIDS:	IT'S REALLY, REALLY, REALLY FUN TO EAT!
COACH:	Shredded Wheat.
CHORUS KIDS:	FUN TO EAT!
ALL:	KELLOGG'S FROSTED MINI-WHEATS.

LEO BURNETT U.S.A.

THE PROCTER & GAMBLE COMPANY
45-Second Film
"WORKOUT"
SECRET SOLID

VIDEO

1 OPEN ON WOMAN IN BEDROOM
PACKING SPORTBAG.

2 REVEAL MAN IN JOGGING SUIT.

3 MOVE IN TO 2-SHOT MAN/WOMAN.

4 SHOT FAVORS MAN IN CU.

5 SCENE CONTINUES 2-SHOT.

6 2-SHOT AS MAN HOLDS UP HIS PRODUCT.

7 SCENE CONTINUES IN 2-SHOT.

8 2-SHOT CONTINUED.

PRUDENTIAL PLAZA • CHICAGO, ILLINOIS 60601
TELEPHONE: (312) 565-5959

As Filmed and Recorded: 12/14/82   sas

AUDIO

SALLY: C'mon, Josh.

JOSH: Sally, I said I'd work out with
you...but <u>not</u> in this.

SALLY: Aw, honey...baby blue's your color.

JOSH: Sal--where I grew up,
wearing baby blue in a gym could
be dangerous.

SALLY: Okay, okay--just hand me my
Secret, huh?

JOSH: Here.

SALLY: Oh, that's yours. I need my
Secret Solid.

JOSH: Now why do we have two antiperspirants?

SALLY: Cause Secret works. And working out
without it could <u>really</u> be dangerous.

LEO BURNETT U.S.A.

<u>VIDEO</u>

9 MAN REACHES TO TRY SECRET.
2-SHOT CONTINUES.

10 ECU OF SECRET APPLICATION.

11 CUT TO MAN SMELLING SECRET.

12 WOMAN BEGINS TO LEAVE BEDROOM.

13 MAN REACHES FOR SECRET.

14 2-SHOT AS WOMAN TAKES HER
PRODUCT AND EXITS

15 CUT TO PRODUCT. WOMAN'S HAND
MOVES MAN'S. SUPER: "STRONG
ENOUGH FOR A MAN"

16 SUPER: "...BUT MADE FOR A WOMAN."
HANDS LEAVE FRAME.

PRUDENTIAL PLAZA • CHICAGO, ILLINOIS 60601
TELEPHONE: (312) 565-5959

AUDIO

JOSH: But my spray's strong.

SALLY: Honey, Secret helps me stay drier...
          and I stay nice to work out next to.

JOSH: Stronger than mine? I'll try it.

SALLY: Josh, Secret's for women...
          goes on silky...dry...and smell.

JOSH: Mmmm...pretty.

SALLY: Not like a guy.

JOSH: Yeah, but if it's strong...

SALLY: Uh, honey...remember...baby blue
          isn't your color.

ANNCR: Secret. Strong enough for a man.

          But made for a woman.

LEO BURNETT U.S.A.

THE PROCTER & GAMBLE COMPANY
45-Second Film
"WEDDING"
SECRET

VIDEO

1   OPEN ON DAD IN HALLWAY OF A HOME.

2   DAD KNOCKS ON DOOR.

3   DOOR OPENS REVEALING ELLEN.

4   CUT TO CU DAD.

5   2-SHOT. ELLEN/DAD.

6   CUT TO BATHROOM AS DAD GOES IN
     AND ELLEN FOLLOWS.

7   2-SHOT. ELLEN/DAD. DAD OFFERS HIS
     SPRAY.

8   CONVERSATION CONTINUES. 2-SHOT.

PRUDENTIAL PLAZA • CHICAGO, ILLINOIS 60601
TELEPHONE: (312) 565-5959

As Filmed and Recorded: 12/14/82   sas

AUDIO

SFX: KNOCK KNOCK

DAD: Ellen! Hurry up. We're going to
          be late!

ELLEN: Relax, Dad. My wedding's four hours
          away.

DAD: Four hours!

DAD: I gotta finish dressing.

ELLEN: Okay, just let me get my Secret
          first.

DAD: Use mine. We'll both need something
          strong today.

ELLEN: No thanks. I need my Secret.

DAD: Oh. Dad's spray isn't good enough
          for you.

ELLEN: Daddy, Secret roll-on works better
          than yours.

LEO BURNETT U.S.A.

VIDEO

9   DAD QUESTIONS 2 ANTIPERSPIRANTS.

10 DAD REACHES FOR PRODUCT.

11 ELLEN DEMONSTRATES SCENT.

12 2-SHOT. DAD/ELLEN. DAD REACHES
    FOR SECRET.

13 ELLEN POLITELY REJECTS DAD.

14 CUT TO LINE SHOT OF SECRET.
    MAN REACHES FOR PRODUCT.
    SUPER: "STRONG ENOUGH FOR
    A MAN"

15 WOMAN'S HAND COMES INTO FRAME AND
    TAKES MAN'S HAND OUT. CONTINUED
    SUPER: "...BUT MADE FOR A WOMAN."

PRUDENTIAL PLAZA • CHICAGO, ILLINOIS 60601
TELEPHONE: (312) 565-5959

AUDIO

DAD: Are you gonna have two antiperspirants
        even after you're married?

ELLEN: Absolutely. Secret really helps
        keep me dry--even when we walk
        down the aisle.

DAD: Don't remind me! Hey, but if it's that
        good...I'll try it.

ELLEN: It's for women. Smell.

DAD: Pretty.

ELLEN: Not like a guy.

DAD: But if...

ELLEN: Sorry, Dad. Don't think of it as
        losing my Secret. Think of it as
        gaining a bathroom.

MAN: (VO) Secret.
        Strong enough for a man.

WOMAN: (VO) But made for a woman.

LEO BURNETT U.S.A.

THE PROCTER & GAMBLE COMPANY
45-Second Film
"THIRTY YEARS"
ALL-TEMPERATURE CHEER
COOLER WATER EMPHASIS

VIDEO

1 OPEN ON MED. SHOT OF SHARI AND MOTHER.
   SHARI HOLDS DIRTY CLOTHES AS MOTHER
   PUTS GROCERIES ON TABLE.

2 SHARI HOLDS UP HER DIRTY BLOUSE.

3 MOTHER TAKES BLOUSE AS SHARI PRESSES
   WARM BUTTON AND SHOWS HER CHEER BOX.

4 MOTHER PRESSES HOT BUTTON.

5 SHARI SHOWS BACK OF CHEER BOX TO
   MOTHER.

PRUDENTIAL PLAZA • CHICAGO, ILLINOIS 60601
TELEPHONE: (312) 565-5959

As Filmed and Recorded: 7/27/81 kjd

<u>AUDIO</u>

MOM: Shari, I haven't dated in thirty
               years!

SHARI: Neither has he.

MOM: But what can I wear?

SHARI: This'll look good.

MOM: But it's dirty.

SHARI: Only until it's washed with All-
               Temperature Cheer in warm water.

               (SFX: PRESSES WARM BUTTON)

MOM: Warm? I can't wear a half washed
               blouse. Use hot.

               (SFX: PRESSES HOT BUTTON)

SHARI: I'm using cooler water now. And that's
               what Cheer cleans in.

LEO BURNETT U.S.A.

VIDEO

6 ECU OF CHEER BACK PANELS. SHARI
   POINTS TO WARM.

7 SHARI PRESSES WARM BUTTON.

8 MOTHER GESTURES TO SHARI.

9 FLIP TO END RESULT. LOTS OF CLEAN
   CLOTHES EVIDENT. MOTHER IS WEARING
   SHARI'S CLEAN BLOUSE.

10 MOTHER PICKS UP CLEAN LAUNDRY
   AND COMMENTS.

11 MOTHER HOLDS UP HER GRANDDAUGHTER'S
   CLEAN DRESS.

12 CHEER BOX IN LIMBO. SUPER: "TOUGH
   ON DIRT."

13 CHEER BOX IN LIMBO. SUPER: "IN
   TODAY'S COOLER TEMPERATURES."

14 CONTINUE SUPER AS "COOLER" POPS
   ON IN LIGHT BLUE.

PRUDENTIAL PLAZA • CHICAGO, ILLINOIS 60601
TELEPHONE: (312) 565-5959

AUDIO

See. Hot, warm--cold.

Cheer's tough on dirt in cooler
temperatures.

MOM: I hope so.

I haven't stood a date up in years.

MOM: Well?

SHARI: You're beautiful.

MOM: Cheer's terrific in warm water.

MOM: Everything looks nice.

SHARI: It'll be like thirty years ago.

MOM: Not quite. Now you can show him
pictures of your grandchildren.

ANNCR: All-Temperature Cheer. Tough on dirt,

in today's

cooler temperatures.

LEO BURNETT U.S.A.

THE PROCTER & GAMBLE COMPANY
45-Second Film
"VACATION II"
ALL-TEMPERATURE CHEER

VIDEO

1   OPEN ON LOIS DOING VACATION LAUNDRY.
    SUITCASE ON DRYER.

2   MC LOIS WITH BATHING SUIT.

3   MC LOIS REACTING TO WEE, PICKING UP
    SUNDRESS.

4   MC LOIS REACTING.

5   CU LOIS WITH SUNDRESS.

6   WEE ZAPS IN CHEER BOX.

7   CU SKEPTICAL LOIS WITH CHEER BOX.

PRUDENTIAL PLAZA • CHICAGO, ILLINOIS 60601
TELEPHONE: (312) 565-5959

As Filmed and Recorded: 6/23/80   ub

AUDIO

WEE: Lois.

LOIS: Aww, go away. I'm still on vacation.

WEE: I let you wear the bikini.

LOIS: Yes and for once I got a decent tan.

WEE: Speaking of decent...

          about that new white dress...

LOIS: It shows off my tan.

WEE: It's not going to stay white that way.

          Help keep it looking new. (ZAP)
          Use All-Temperature Cheer and the
          right temperature.

LOIS: Temperatures don't matter.

LEO BURNETT U.S.A.

VIDEO

8 WEE "ZAPS" IN DRESS WASHED THE CHEER WAY.

9 MS LOIS EXAMINING DRESS.

10 WEE ZAPS IN DRESS WASHED THE WRONG WAY.

11 CU LOIS EXAMINING DRESS.

12 CU OF BOX TOP.

13 MS LOIS WITH CLEAN CLOTHES.

14 MC LOIS REACTING TO WEE.

15 ANIMATED CAMPAIGN SEQUENCE ENDED.
   SUPER: "ALL TEMPERATURE CHEER.
   HELPS KEEP CLOTHES LOOKING NEW."

16 SUPER: "ALL TEMPA-CHEER."

PRUDENTIAL PLAZA • CHICAGO, ILLINOIS 60601
TELEPHONE: (312) 565-5959

AUDIO

WEE:	Oh? Look. (ZAP) This dress was dirtied and washed five times the Cheer way--in the right temperature--hot.
LOIS:	It's about as white as mine.
WEE:	But look (ZAP) after five washings your way.
LOIS:	It's still dirty.
WEE:	See? Cheer in the right temperature helps keep clothes looking new.
LOIS:	I like washing in hot, warm, cold. My clothes look nice. And my white dress is going to knock his eyes out.
WEE:	Not if I can help it.
ANNCR:	All-Temperature Cheer. (ZAP) Helps keep your clothes looking new.
	All Tempa-Cheer.

LEO BURNETT U.S.A.

THE PROCTER & GAMBLE COMPANY
30-Second Film
"PRACTICED FINGERS - LONG HAIR"
LILT

VIDEO

1   SPOT OPENS IN HAIRDRESSER'S SALON.
    CAMERA TRAVELS INTO THE SET FRAMING
    WOMEN WORKING ON CLIENTS.

2   THE CAMERA TRAVEL SHOT DISCOVERS
    THE SPOKESMAN AS HE WORKS ON A
    HEAD OF WOMAN. HE LOOKS AT CAMERA.

3   CUT TO TIGHT SHOT OF SPOKESMAN AS
    HE STOPS WHAT HE IS DOING AND TALKS
    TO CAMERA.

4   THE SPOKESMAN MOVES HIS FINGERS TO
    ACCENT "ROLL-UPS."

5   SIDE BY SIDE DEMO. SHOWING RESULTS
    FROM GOOD AND BAD ROLL-UPS. SUPER
    TISSUES.

6   CUT TO CU OF SPONGES AND PRODUCT
    BOX ON DRESSER. A WOMAN'S HAND
    TAKES A SPONGE.

7   DISSOLVE TO CU OF FINGERS DOING A
    ROLL-UP.

PRUDENTIAL PLAZA • CHICAGO, ILLINOIS 60601
TELEPHONE: (312) 565-5959

As Filmed and Recorded: 06/27/83   sas

AUDIO

MUSIC: SFX

HAIRDRESSER: A touch for making hair look beautiful

...takes years of practice. But
when you perm at home, you can have
that touch too, with Lilt.

You see...it's all in the roll-ups.

A bad roll-up show frizzies...
A good roll-up...beautiful curls.

Only Lilt has these amazing sponges.

They grip better, roll up better

LEO BURNETT U.S.A.

VIDEO

8 DISSOLVE TO WOMAN WITH BEAUTIFUL
   HEAD OF HAIR.

9 THE WOMAN TOUCHES HER HAIR WITH
   HER FINGERS.

10 CUT BACK TO SPOKESMAN IN SALON
   AS HE SPEAKS TO CAMERA. HE HAS
   A TWINKLE IN HIS EYE.

11 DISSOLVE TO FINAL PRODUCT BEAUTY
   SHOT.

PRUDENTIAL PLAZA • CHICAGO, ILLINOIS 60601
TELEPHONE: (312) 565-5959

AUDIO

for more beautiful hair.

Lilt's sponges put a professional
touch right at your fingertips...

And I had to practice for years.

ANNCR: LILT'S Professional touch...
          Beautiful.

Appendix B

Offices of SAG and AFTRA

Locations of offices are presented in alphabetical order, first by state, and then, within each state, by city. To find the specific geographical area covered by a particular office, contact the office directly.

Reasonable effort has been made in the accurate compilation of the information contained herein; the author, publisher, and respective union, however, assume no liability for errors or omissions.

SCREEN ACTORS GUILD

National Office
7750 Sunset Blvd.
Hollywood, CA 90046
(213) 876-3030

Arizona
3030 N. Central, #919
Phoenix, AZ 85012
(602) 279-9975

California
3045 Rosecrans, #308
San Diego, CA 92110
(714) 222-3996

100 Bush St., 26th Floor
San Francisco, CA 94104
(415) 391-7510

Colorado
6825 E. Tennessee Ave., #639
Denver, CO 80222
(303) 388-4287

Florida
145 Madeira Ave., #317
Coral Gables, FL 33134
(305) 444-7677

Georgia
3110 Maple Dr., N.E., #210
Atlanta, GA 30305
(404) 237-9961

Illinois
307 N. Michigan Ave.
Chicago, IL 60601
(312) 372-8081

Maryland (serves DC & VA)
35 Wisconsin Circle, #210
Chevy Chase, MD 20815
(301) 657-2560

Massachusetts
11 Beacon St., #1000
Boston, MA 02108
(617) 742-2688

Michigan
28690 Southfield Rd.
Lathrup Village, MI 48076
(313) 559-9540

Minnesota
2500 Park Ave., Ste. A*
Minneapolis, MN 55402
(612) 871-2404

Missouri
406 W. 34th St., #310*
Kansas City, MO 64111
(816) 753-4557

818 Olive St., #1237*
St. Louis, MO 63101
(314) 231-8410

New York
1700 Broadway, 18th Floor
New York, NY 10019
(212) 957-5370

Ohio
1367 E. 6th St.*
Cleveland, OH 44114
(216) 781-2255

Pennsylvania
1405 Locust St., #811
Philadelphia, PA 19102
(215) 545-3150

Tennessee
P.O. Box 121087
Nashville, TN 37212
(615) 327-2944

Texas
3220 Lemmon Ave., #102
Dallas, TX 75204
(214) 522-2080

2620 Fountainview, #215
Houston, TX 77057
(713) 972-1806

Washington
158 Thomas St.*
Seattle, WA 98109
(206) 624-7340

*AFTRA offices which handle SAG for their area.

AMERICAN FEDERATION OF TELEVISION AND RADIO ARTISTS

National Office

Sanford I. Wolff, Esq., National Exec. Sec.
1350 Avenue of the Americas
New York, NY 10019
(212) 265-7700

Locals and Chapters

Arizona

Mr. Donald Livesay, Exec. Sec.
3030 N. Central, #301
Phoenix, AZ 85012
(602) 279-9975

California

Kenneth Clarke, Pres.
4418 E. Austin Way
Fresno, CA 93726
(209) 224-8929

Mr. H. Wayne Oliver, Exec. Sec.
1717 N. Highland Ave.
Hollywood, CA 90028
(213) 461-8111

Hirsch Adell, Esq.
Reich, Adell, & Crost
501 Shatto Place, #100
Los Angeles, CA 90020
(213) 386-3860

Mr. James E. Zewe, Pres.
822 Terrace Place, Apt. D
Madera, CA 93637
(209) 674-1039

Ms. Jacqueline Walters, Exec. Sec.
3045 Rosecrans St., #308
San Diego, CA 92110
(619) 222-1161

AFTRA offices (continued)

Ms. Carol Thorp, Pres.
c/o KOVR-TV
1216 Arden Way
Sacramento, CA 95815
(916) 927-1313

Donald S. Tayer, Esq., Exec. Sec.
   and Counsel
100 Bush St., 15th Floor
San Francisco, CA 94104
(415) 391-7510

Colorado
Jerre Hookey, Exec. Sec.
6825 E. Tennessee, #639
Denver, CO 80224
(303) 388-4287

Connecticut
Mr. Len Gambino, Steward
c/o Station WSTC
117 Prospect St.
Stamford, CT 06901
(203) 327-1400

District of Columbia
Mr. Don Gaynor, Exec. Sec.
35 Wisconsin Circle, #210
Chevy Chase, MD 20815
(serves DC, MD, & VA)

Florida
Ms. Diane Hogan, Asst. Exec. Sec.
1450 N.E. 123rd St., #102
North Miami, FL 33161
(305) 891-0779

Georgia
Mr. Thomas Even, Exec. Sec.
3110 Maple Dr. N.E., #210
Atlanta, GA 30305
(404) 237-0831; (404) 237-9961

Hawaii
Ms. Brenda Chayra
P.O. Box 1350
Honolulu, HI 96807
(808) 533-2652

Illinois
Mr. Herb Neuer, Exec. Sec.
307 N. Michigan Ave.
Chicago, IL 60601
(312) 372-8081

Seymour Schriar, Esq.
29 S. LaSalle St.
Chicago, IL 60603
(312) 346-0252

Mr. Thomas MacIntyre, Pres.
Station WEEK
2907 Springfield Rd.
East Peoria, IL 61611
(309) 699-5052

Indiana
Mr. Irving Fink, Exec. Sec.
Yosha & Cline
2220 N. Meridian St.
Indianapolis, IN 46204
(317) 635-5395

Kentucky
Mr. John V. Hanley, Exec. Sec.
730 W. Main St., #250
Louisville, KY 40202
(502) 584-6594

Louisiana
Ms. Pauline Morgan, Exec. Sec.
808 St. Anne
New Orleans, LA 70116
(504) 524-9903

Maryland
Mr. Don Gaynor, Exec. Sec.
35 Wisconsin Circle, #210
Chevy Chase, MD 20815
(301) 657-2560

Bernard Rubenstein, Esq.
10 Light St., #1145
Baltimore, MD 21202
(301) 752-6160

AFTRA Offices (continued)

Massachusetts
Mr. Robert Segal, Exec. Sec.
11 Beacon St., #1000
Boston, MA 02108
(617) 742-0208; (617) 742-2688

Michigan
Ms. Mary Ann Formaz, Exec. Sec.
24901 North Western Hwy.
Heritage Plaza Office Bldg., #406
Southfield, MI 48075
(313) 354-1774

Minnesota
Mr. John Kailin, Exec. Sec.
2500 Park Avenue South, Ste. A
Minneapolis, MN 55404
(612) 871-2404

Missouri
Ms. Caroline Noble, Exec. Sec.
406 W. 34th St., #310
Kansas City, MO 64111
(816) 753-4557

Mr. Larry Ward, Exec. Sec.
Paul Brown Bldg.
818 Olive St., #1237
St. Louis, MO 63101
(314) 231-8410

New York
Mr. Jim Gagliardi, Steward
c/o Station WROW-AM
341 Northern Blvd.
Albany, NY 12204
(518) 436-4841

Mr. Doug Meyers
c/o Station WTEN-TV
341 Northern Blvd.
Albany, NY 12201
(518) 436-4822

Mr. Bob Buchanan, Steward
c/o Station WBNG-TV
50 Front St.
Binghamton, NY 13905
(607) 723-7311

Mr. Stanford M. Silverberg, Exec. Sec.
Silverberg, Silverberg, Yood, & Sellers
635 Brisbane Bldg.
Buffalo, NY 14203
(716) 854-6495

Ms. Marie Rice, Pres.
c/o WIVB-TV
2077 Elmwood Ave.
Buffalo, NY 14207
(716) 874-4410

Mortimer Becker, Esq.
Becker & London
30 Lincoln Plaza, Mezz. Floor
New York, NY 10023
(212) 541-7070

Mr. Reginald Dowell, Exec. Sec.
1350 Avenue of the Americas
2nd Floor
New York, NY 10019
(212) 265-7700

Ms. Marcia Boyd, Exec. Sec.
One Exchange St., #900
Rochester, NY 14614
(716) 232-1540

Mr. Jim Leonard, Pres.
170 Ray Avenue
Schenectady, NY 12304
(518) 385-1267

Ohio
Ms. Sharyl Rosen, Administratc
1814-16 Carew Tower
Cincinnati, OH 45202
(513) 579-8668

Mr. Kenneth Bichl, Exec. Sec.
1367 E. 6th St.
#229, The Lincoln Bldg.
Cleveland, OH 44114
(216) 781-2255

Oregon
Mr. Robert Dolton, Exec. Sec.
915 N.E. Davis St.
Portland, OR 97232
(503) 238-6914

AFTRA Offices (continued)

Pennsylvania

Mr. Glenn A. Goldstein, Exec. Sec.
1405 Locust St., #811
Philadelphia, PA 19102
(215) 732-0507

Mr. Dan Mallinger, Exec. Sec.
625 Stanwix St., The Penthouse
Pittsburgh, PA 15222
(412) 281-6767

Tennessee

Mr. David Maddox, Exec. Sec.
P.O. Box 121087
1108 17th Ave. South
Nashville, TN 37212
(615) 327-2947; (615) 327-2944

Texas

Ms. Betty Boyer, Exec. Sec.
3220 Lemmon Ave., #102
Dallas, TX 75204
(214) 522-2080; (214) 522-2085

Ms. Claire Gordon, Exec. Sec.
2620 Fountainview, #214
Houston, TX 77057
(713) 972-1806

Washington

Ms. Carol Matt, Exec. Sec.
P.O. Box 9688
158 Thomas St.
Seattle, WA 98109
(206) 624-7340

Harold Green, Esq.
MacDonald, Hoague & Bayless
2nd Ave. & Cherry St.
Seattle, WA 98104
(206) 622-1604

Wisconsin

Ms. Irene Nelson
929 52nd St.
Kenosha, WI 53140

Appendix C

Other Avenues for Making Money

Voice-Overs & Radio Ads

Voice-over actors are actors who talk, but who aren't seen, though many actors who do voice-over work also do on-camera acting. Next time you're in front of the tube, watch some commercials and you'll hear announcers whom you don't see.

One advantage of voice-over work is that you can *sometimes* have product conflicts that are legal. You usually aren't as associated with the product in a voice-over as you are when you're in front of the camera. BUT, the general rule of thumb is that the voices between two competing products must not be identifiable with each other. In other words, if you did a character voice in one ad, and a straight voice in the competing ad, this might be perfectly legal. However, you must clear this product conflict with the companies you're working for.

There's a lot of work for voice-over actors—commercials, cartoons, TV narration, and radio, to name some possibilities. Voice-over work calls for a very specialized talent, and you really have to be able to use your voice well to get cast in this field. In the larger markets, generally it's not a field that the beginner can "jump right into," but rather a field where proven professionals are used. In the smaller markets the odds increase for less experienced actors to get voice-over work.

Many of the principles used in getting work as a visible actor generally apply to obtaining work as a voice-over actor (radio and otherwise). For instance, one still must obtain an agent, and the differences between obtaining an agent for the voice-over areas as opposed to the other acting fields are outlined below.

Most voice-over agents are associated with commercial agents. In other words, some big commercial agencies have a separate department specifically for voice-over work. Simply check with commercial agents and ask if they have a voice-over department. To seek representation, phone first and try to set up appointments. If they won't see you, which is usually the case, especially in the Major Cities, then mail your resume and tape to them. *Do not make a tape that sounds homemade!* If you do the recording yourself, make sure it sounds professional. An amateur-sounding recording is to the voice-over industry what a bad photograph is to the theatrical industry: it does more harm than good. Do readings of material that suit your voice best—commercial readings, animated voices, etc. The tape should be *reel-to-reel* and shouldn't be over five minutes in length.

This tape is your passport to the voice-over industry as photographs are to the acting industry. Once you have an agent, he'll be submitting this tape to voicecasters (casting directors for voice-over work) for potential jobs. Many times the voicecaster will send the material he wants read to your agent. Your agent will have a few actors in to record the material for the voicecaster; most voice-over agents have reel-to-reel machines in their offices and recordings for a specific job can be recorded right there. Other times you might go to the voicecaster's or the ad agency's office to audition.

Print Work

Print work really comes under the modeling category, but it is in some ways connected to commercial acting. There are many different types of print work—magazine and newspaper ads, bill-boards, posters, etc. Many actors/models are used for the above media.

The general conception is that the actor/model has to be of the glamorous type to be in the print media. This couldn't be further from the truth. "Commercial print" is one of the biggest areas of the print market. These types of ads use everyday-looking people. How many times have you seen ads, for example, for McDonald's, Coke, Kentucky Fried Chicken, American Airlines, etc., using the "girl or guy next door"?

Many commercial agents also have print departments, especially in the smaller markets. Agents in the smaller markets have to cover more areas of the profession because there might not be enough work in one category to keep them afloat. So in the smaller markets it will be much easier to detect which agents do print work and which do not than it will be in the larger markets where many agents specialize.

Print agents do not come under the jurisdiction of SAG or AFTRA, unless they happen to be handling people for film and tape representation also, and even then SAG and AFTRA have no jurisdiction over what the agency does with its print department. So when dealing with print agents you're pretty much on your own. They can charge whatever percentage they want. Most charge between ten and fifteen percent. However, as with all agents, you shouldn't pay any print agent any money until you work, and then only a percentage of the amount you're paid for that job. Any contracts with print agents should be read carefully since the contracts aren't standard.

One way to find out about print agents in the major markets is to obtain a list of agents from SAG, as prescribed earlier. Look for the agents that handle actors commercially. (The list denotes what areas the agents represent.) Then phone and agents and ask whoever answers the phone if that agency has a print department.

Of course, you should check around with your actor friends to see which agencies would be right for you in this department.

Many print agents do not handle actors for film and tape, so they won't appear on the SAG list. Many of these print agents are highly specialized and extremely good, so be sure to check around with actors, models, other agents, photographers, etc., to find out about them. Once you've been in a particular city for a short period of time, you'll begin to learn about agents and their specialties.

You can have a different agent for print work than you do for commercials or you can have the same for both. Most print agents use the actor's commercial composite for commercial print. In the modeling field many agents use "zed cards" instead of composites, but you should consult another book for that field, since we're dealing with commercial print only.

Print work is a great outlet for the commercial actor. There are rarely any type of use payments (i.e., residuals), but the hourly pay is usually very good. And, you never know when print work can lead to other jobs. For example, my print agent sent me on a billboard ad interview for Kodak. It so happened that the same people who were casting the print ad were also casting the TV commercial. In other words, they were working on a large campaign. Though I was not picked to do the billboard ad, I was selected to be in the TV commercial. (My commercial agent ended up with the commission since I was signed to her for commercials and my print agent was kind enough to refuse any commission; I bought her a box of chocolate candies which she probably preferred.) This is a rare occurence, but the point is that this is definitely a field you should check into while working on your TV commercial career.

About the Author

Tom Logan was born in Shreveport, Louisiana. His acting debut was at age 8, in Shreveport, where he performed in plays until he graduated from high school and left town to begin his college education. He performed in over 50 community theater and college stage productions at such places as Centenary College, the University of Arkansas, the University of California at Santa Barbara, and California State University in Northridge. He graduated cum laude from the latter, with a B.A. degree in Theatre Arts.

In between his various college enrollments, Tom performed in many professional stage productions, among them "Applause" and "Mame" in the state of New York, and "You're a Good Man, Charlie Brown" playing Schroeder, and "Androcles and the Lion" playing Androcles; with the latter two he toured.

Wishing to break into motion pictures and TV, Logan moved to California. His movie credits include a starring role in "Breakthrough," a co-starring role in "Massacre at Central High" (*New York Times* 20 Best Films List, 1980), and appearances in several other films. He has had co-starring or feature parts in episodes of many prime-time TV series, including "CHiPs" (NBC), "What's Happening" (ABC), and "CPO Sharkey" (NBC). Tom has also acted in a made-for-television movie and on

175

the soap operas "General Hospital," "Days of Our Lives," and "The Young and the Restless."

Logan is well qualified to write on the art and the business of performing in TV commercials. He has held principal roles in many national commercials, for companies including McDonald's, Ford, Honda, Coppertone, and Kodak. From that experience, Tom has learned numerous techniques for succeeding in the commercial acting field. He passes along many of these "secrets" in ACTING IN THE MILLION DOLLAR MINUTE.

In addition to his acting jobs, Tom has experience in helping others to master the fundamentals of commercial acting and launch their own careers. He teaches and lectures on acting in TV commercials to students at various studios in Los Angeles, and with the American Film Institute in L.A. and other cities. His first book, HOW TO ACT & EAT AT THE SAME TIME, is an encouraging and practical guide to landing a professional acting job.